Caring for M

By

Anne Carpenter

Dedication

I have been part of a community I have never met, whose lives have been taken over by the needs of someone they love. I don't know who they are or where they are but I acknowledge them with humility.

Prologue

I'm sitting in the crematorium right at the front, dressed in black. I wanted to sit at the back so I could observe everyone else but they said I had to sit at the front and now everyone else is observing me and perhaps they look for clues to detect how I am feeling. They might even examine whether their own level of sadness is appropriate; is it guiltily little or surprisingly overwhelming? Perhaps their minds jump about amongst their memories of her, throwing up random pictures, phrases and emotions, recreations of a moment with her long ago. Do any of the individual memories collide, are there two people remembering the same moment with her, how many moments of her life are here in the room creating a fantastic invisible kaleidoscope of her life?

It is a beautiful, perfectly clean room, pine and white. If you stand at the back by the double doors you can see a pine clad aisle with quiet ranks of pine pews on each side of it and the aisle opening out to an expanse of shiny floor on which stand two huge bouquets of flowers on pine columns. The flowers look real but I can't be sure. To your right is the lectern and double doors leading outside and to the left is the high plinth for the coffin, the very last resting place, draped to the floor in black fabric and a burgundy curtain to draw against our sensitivity as the plinth doors open leading to the very end. It is barren as a room but the facing wall is a huge window showing a glorious view across green fields to autumn woodland on the slopes of the hills with the sun glancing over the red, orange and amber of the trees. What a pity she has missed this view, she would have loved it.

Our huge family, our tribe, fill the pews. My brother Kit is sitting next to me and my husband Joe behind with Roz, my sister. It was Kit who came to the funeral parlour with me. Mother was in the building somewhere, in some kind of fridge I imagine, but I had no sense of her. I didn't want to see her; I saw my other sister when she was dead and it wasn't like they say in novels, she didn't look at peace. Mother had made all the arrangements at least a decade ago and despite the inflation in the intervening years the price had still been honoured by Age UK and the whole process was handled with such ease thanks to the funeral director. The only part that was odd was when we were asked to choose the light or dark wood for the coffin and warned off the wicker model because it squeaked and groaned when moved. Can you imagine! You might think your loved one had changed their mind about dying and was trying to get out.

When the funeral director phoned the organist it turned out Mother had arranged that too, as she was acquainted with him through village life, and he had remembered her strict instructions to play 'something not too solemn'. At the time this alarmed me ever so slightly in case she had ordered a medley of wartime songs, which were actually her favourite musical diet, and I began to imagine 'I'll Be Seeing You' or 'We'll Meet Again' wafting across the crematorium which might have been unnerving for the congregation. My suspicion is averted as I can hear an electric organ now at the back of the room. The organ notes are barely audible, long, extended, tuneless and then open out into a turgid melody. Something is beginning and the sound gathers up the disparate thoughts into focus, brings us all together in one accord, so that the air is heavy now with mourners, hushed, reverent, fearful.

I can't stop sobbing. I have to put my fist against my mouth to stop any noise coming out and upsetting other people. Kit has passed me a cotton handkerchief. Joe has his hand on my shoulder. They're singing a hymn now. The heavy, ponderous sound is inside my head and far away at the same time and I am struggling to control my breathing. I have to get control because soon the black frocked vicar will nod to me and I will have to get up, and walk to the lectern on shaking knees to give the eulogy.

That's what she wanted, for me to write the eulogy because, being the first born, I have known her the longest time, longer than anyone in this room. I was aware that, by choosing me the, part of her life in which I and my father featured, when she was at her happiest, would be counted. I am the only person who knew about life before Max, her second husband, not that she didn't love the children she and Max had together, it was just that they only knew life after Max.

I have wondered if after Max died, some ten years ago, she found some personal authority, some revaluing of self, freedom to do exactly what she wanted, something she had not felt for many years, because in her papers I found, just before she died, a note hand written in pencil and fastened to her funeral arrangements with a paper clip. It said 'In the paper with the order of service I wish to have a photo of me on my own.' The last three words were underlined.

I was going through the papers because I thought I might find something to help me write the eulogy; she always kept odd little bits of memorabilia, press cuttings, letters, cards, that kind of thing. I found a stack of beautiful love letters from my father, written from the battlefields of the second world war before he was blown to smithereens by a mine ten days before the so called victory. There were newspaper photos of the sinking of the Ark Royal, her brother grinning through the dots of the newsprint in the group of rescued sailors. There was a creased permit card authorising her to attend at first aid posts as a part time red cross nurse, several yellowed and fragile newspaper reviews of her many appearances in local amateur dramatics and numerous good references from head teachers as she moved through her life as a teacher. Nobody has ever seen these little scruffy, faded scraps that evidence the bounty of her one hundred and one years.

And here is where it ends, in this place built for death which has no congruence with her life. I am shocked by it all. Earlier, as the black limousine we travelled in pulled up behind the hearse, I saw the light wood coffin. She was in there. I hadn't thought of that before. She was in the coffin and it looked too small, too narrow. They lifted her so easily, as if she weighed nothing at all, and carried her in and laid her down on the plinth with utter reverence, with absolute respect, although they didn't know her. So there lies my Mother in a tiny box where so many mothers must have laid before, enduring the outpourings of their bereaved families and friends.

I glance to my left and see the family she cherished so much, the three generations, ranging from me through to a child probably not yet even announced, a child to know her only through the stories fondly told. Each one of this dear tribe knowing only a part of her, their own special and exclusive part, and nobody ever knowing the whole. Perhaps I do know more than all these others. Perhaps I am the right one to give the eulogy.

I look up and catch the eye of the vicar. He is nodding to me. I walk up to the lectern and the vicar points out the microphone and I say 'I don't need a microphone'. It is a genuine and automatic reaction but it probably sounds arrogant. He would not suggest I use the microphone if he knew me. I see several people in the congregation smile because they do know me. They know I have spent my working life as an actor, have played theatres with stalls, boxes, grand circles and balconies with out a microphone. The vicar is a stranger invading our close knit gathering.

I immediately feel a turmoil inside because I have already had a subdued argument with him and been hurt by it. Mother wanted a simple Christian ceremony but he had argued with the family's choice of a Christian hymn, my sister Roz reading one of her poems written especially for the funeral and Mother's favourite song from primary school teaching days, 'Glad that I live am I', sung as a solo by her grandson's wife. The vicar had said it was 'canon law' that we had certain readings and prayers and I wondered what penal recrimination there would be for me if I broke a Canon law; perhaps a thunderbolt would strike me down. I felt a burning in my chest again because he didn't know my Mother, he didn't know what she intended for her service and I did because I knew her, I knew exactly what she wanted. The beautifully simple service we had designed for Mother was being taken over. You may think I'm over reacting and perhaps I am, but it isn't easy for anyone, especially when they are threatened with the strong arm of the Canon Law. I have a bad history with the clergy. I'm not sure whether to tell you that story later, I might.

Chapter One

QUANTUM LEAP

I have just made my seventh return journey from Manchester to Cornwall so far this year and I need to do some serious thinking. Last Christmas Mother fell and injured her leg whilst putting up her Christmas decorations. I am not sure how, at the age of ninety four, she had been allowed by friends and family to do this by herself, but knowing Mother's determination and her refusal to let age curtail her, I can imagine that the first they knew was when somebody called and found her in pain and distress but determined to 'manage'. When I got there in the new year her ankle was still badly swollen and she was barely able to look after herself and I wished that somebody had taken her to hospital to properly discover what the injury was and make sure appropriate treatment was in place. If anybody has suggested this she would probably have told them not to bother as she was all right.

I was happy to make the journey to look after her until she was mobile enough to bring her back to Manchester with me for a final recuperation. I was aware that this was probably her last visit to my home city and I planned to make it a good one.

Fortunately my daughter was free and volunteered to do the driving to get us back to Manchester and run us around and Mother asked us to hire a car that she could get into easily; she willingly paid the cost because, although in many ways she is frugal, she does have spare money and was delighted to spend it on a posh car in which to drive ostentatiously through the village on her way up north. There was a slight hiatus on the journey when we got to Exeter and Mother realised she had forgotten her hat and she needed some persuasion to agree that it was too far to turn back and she could buy a new hat in Manchester.

It is only recently that she has needed to be driven to make her way from her house to mine, a distance of three hundred miles. In her younger day she had never learnt to drive and always regretted the privacy and independence she missed because of it, but she would come on the train and think nothing of it. Then even a journey with assistance offered by the railway staff became too difficult, too long and too tiring. Later we persuaded her to fly from Cornwall to Manchester, with one side of the family delivering her to her departure airport and another meeting her at the destination. This she loved. Mother had never flown anywhere before and she loved being in the air, getting there so fast and, most of all, how smart and sophisticated she found herself. But those days have also passed and now she needs to be driven.

Once at my home we commandeered my grandson to push the wheelchair, which he enjoyed doing and with his usual diligence became a master of manoeuvring, my daughter did the driving and the four of us had a real city break in the best of cities. So she shopped at Harvey Nicks, she toured the Peak District, she had her photo taken next to a Dalek at Media City and she experienced the 3D cinema at the Science and Industry Museum. To cap it all she had cocktails in the stylish Sky Bar, twenty three floors up at the Hilton, where she sat among the on-trend Mancunians sipping champagne in her best Scottish Wool Shop outfit. I will always be glad that we did it because it was never to happen again, we knew that.

Mother has always viewed Christmas through rose tinted spectacles and no matter what her circumstances she has tried to make it a big event. When we were a large growing family all the traditions were observed; we each had a stir of the pudding months before, coins were pressed into the sticky mix, she made mince pies to die for, paper chains were stuck together and pinned to cornices, trees potted and decorated and stockings hung and filled and emptied before a gargantuan feast.

Now there are no children in her home, no grandchildren even and although someone will always invite her to Christmas dinner she returns to an empty house. She is not willing to let go of her memories of six healthy children round the Christmas dinner table wearing paper hats and pulling crackers and flushed with excitement over new toys and Christmas cheer. But this is not the family that she has today; there are grandchildren and great grandchildren in plenty, but of her original six children one, my beloved sister, is sadly deceased, one estranged and one unlikely to return from abroad. We are virtually a small family now, just Roz and Kit and myself but at least if Joe and I do decide to move, we all three of us would live within a reasonable distance of her.

However, still the tree must go up, the wreath hung on the door and the glass angels hung in the window in the precise positions they have always occupied for the twelve days and traditional food must be eaten. Mince pies now come from Sainsburys and not from her kitchen and the giant turkey is more likely to be a few slices of turkey breast in a plastic package. The cards still come in and are blue tacked to the kitchen dresser and she counts them to see if she has more or less than last year. Less could mean yet another friend has died. She clings to the charade.

During the year that has just passed, after her last visit to Manchester, she has fallen in the kitchen, fallen in the garden, been rushed to hospital twice with a stomach problem and each time I have dropped everything to go there and each time I have seen her look weaker, have more difficulty walking and become more frightened of what might happen as she continues to live alone; she can't even lift the kettle now to make a cup of tea. I have shared the care of Mother with my sister Roz; two weeks on, two weeks off mostly and it has left the chaos of neglect in both our homes and every time Roz and I met or spoke on the phone we had asked the question, and every time we had no answer. Roz suggested tentatively that was a nice care home near her, and we said 'mmm...'

The logistics of getting her around are increasingly difficult; I am not a happy driver and, whilst I don't mind chugging around Manchester on familiar roads in my beat up Ford Fiesta, I'm scared of driving the three hundred miles to Mother's house. I did do it, just once, in my last and favourite ever car, a red cinquecento, but I had to be towed most of the way back by the RAC. Three hundred miles in the company of a burly lorry driver with poor communication skills. It kind of put me off. I'm pretty sure that if I tried it again I would have wall to wall panic attacks. Anyway I really like trains, especially when they are on time. I used to go to a grammar school forty miles from my home by steam train. I really miss the carriages

3

with scratchy upholstery, net luggage racks and sliding doors onto corridors. Long carriages are just not the same, no romance about them.

The trouble with doing the journey by train is that when I get to Mother's house I have no transport so we are rather stuck in the house or limited by how far I can push her in the wheelchair. There are taxis and I have used them on occasion but they are very expensive. We took a taxi once up to the cliff top where there is a little café so that Mother could gaze over the sea. She used to walk along these cliffs, even in her late eighties she would stride along for miles up the steepest of inclines and over rough surfaces and often I have had a job to keep up with her. When she had gazed long enough and eaten well I decided to call a taxi to get home but could not find a signal anywhere, until someone called out to me that 'the signal' was a few yards down the cliff path by the bench, and sure enough it was. This is the price you pay for the beauty of ocean, hills and valleys!

On one of my visits over the last year she had a routine dental appointment, the dentist being seven miles away, so we took another expensive taxi. I was worried about how Mother would manage the examination but rather than move her onto the dentist's chair, which I thought might have involved a lot of cumbersome lifting, the dentist examined her in the wheelchair and luckily found no problems. Some of Mother's teeth, the front ones, are false. It's very odd because they don't look anything like her own teeth which were just like her father's, my beloved grandad's teeth, proper family teeth, and now she has neat, small, very white front teeth which lack the character of her real ones. One of my dear aunties had all their teeth extracted for free when the national health first started. Apparently it was quite a normal thing to do in those days and consequently she has never had to pay a dentist's bill. Sounds good.

Mother really enjoyed the trip even though the destination was the dentist surgery. She enjoys any kind of medical intervention that isn't too painful and it helped that the dentist was a handsome and kindly young man with a charming foreign accent, Romanian I believe.

This lovely dentist might encourage me to sign up. I have a horrible history with teeth. My milk teeth decided they quite liked living where they were and by the age of thirty were more or less collapsed and a dentist decided to take them out and replace them with a denture. I was on stage one night when my denture fell out. I managed to catch it and shove it back into my mouth and I still don't know whether the audience noticed. I didn't hear anyone laugh. The denture was replaced by a bridge. A bridge ruins all the real teeth it is fixed to, I'm warning you because they don't tell you that beforehand in case you decide to avoid paying. My bridge will soon have to come out. I feel I have outlived my teeth. Every day that passes without a toothache is a day gained. I can't look at my teeth in the mirror, I am in denial.

***

I didn't need transport last time Mother was taken off to hospital while I was on my caring shift because I went with her in the ambulance and managed to get a convenient bus home, quite an achievement in a rural area. It was her stomach this time, acute pain which she couldn't bear. She actually asked to go to hospital which convinced me to dial 999 because she isn't one for making a fuss and normally puts up with pain well, and the decision was confirmed when even the chatting and good humour of the ambulance crew didn't cheer her.

I was on the ward when the specialist came round followed by a huddle of student doctors. He was a portly gent with a little ginger goatee beard and his examination and diagnosis was pure theatre; I believe he must have watched the Doctor in the House films and modelled his delivery on James Robertson Justice. He pontificated over lower left quadrants and diverticula with elaborate gestures for his attentive audience. Mother was very keen to be involved in the drama and began to make her own suggestions in her best posh teacher voice and I saw the students attempting to hide their grins as she told the consultant his business. On her way through life Mother has picked up a couple of medical terms which she likes to bandy about, her favourite being 'the sacroiliac' to which is attributed many a woe, but although on this occasion she could not use this specialist

5

knowledge, she gave the consultant a run for his money and a story for the student doctors to relate later.

Of course everybody in the street had seen the ambulance so there was no need to explain to anyone why Mother had been absent, in fact an ambulance usually promoted a guessing game as to who's turn it was, since there were several elderly or infirm clients nearby. The old lady in Primrose cottage across the road is well known to the emergency service. Mother's friend Madge lives with her husband Leo two doors down and both of them are elderly. Leo is a familiar sight in the village as he takes a walk through the same route twice a day, regular as clockwork, wearing a jaunty cap and carrying a small knapsack on his back and calling in at the Co-Op for a ready meal. Twice a day we hear his stick tap - tapping as he passes Mother's window.

Madge only leaves the house to go to the hairdresser and to visit Mother. She is a very private person but she shares Mother's interest in gardening and watching the bullocks on the field and is also an ex-teacher and since Mother still gets about a little in the village she is able to relay to Madge the latest gossip. All of them are regulars at the district hospital.

***

A decision about what to do with Mother has to be made before a tragedy occurs but it is hard. Instinctively I want to go, I like the country side and village life, but I like Manchester too. The two environments are worlds apart with totally different good experiences to offer.

My house would be impossible for Mother. It is a solid little house, sensible Northern red brick, mid terrace, circa 1900, built for mill workers in the heart of a once great industrial city; the conventional two up two down with kitchen extension and attic room. We can't bring her here; nowhere to put a stair lift and not enough rooms. I'm not sure how my husband Joe feels about it. We are devoted to our four cats; Mother has tolerated rather than loved pets and I'm not sure she would be able to show our darlings the kind of respect they have become accustomed to.

We've been here in this Manchester house for thirty years, everything is exactly how we want it, budget allowing. It is small but entirely efficient, everything works, all the light bulbs are LEDs, everything is at peak economy and as environmentally friendly as we can get it. We have a very efficient and cosy central heating system. I have often said I would like to lift my house up just as it is and replant it in the countryside. I have spent years creating a charming courtyard garden and a really lovely allotment close by. Bits and pieces of acting work are still coming in and there are friends and colleagues I have known for many years from my work in theatre and as a singer. My allotment friends don't think I should give it up. They are Northerners, they don't mince their words, they don't think I should go.

And then there's her house. It's the same size as our house except without a separate kitchen and on the end of a terrace of cottages but in a totally different setting; she is on the edge of a village in a rural community. Most of it is the original ancient stone with deep window sills, circa probably sixteenth century with additions and subtractions over hundreds of years. An estate agent would say 'A quirky country cottage with uninterrupted rural views set in a desirable village and with parking for one car.' For heating there is a small coal fire and two other rooms have storage heaters that are stifling at breakfast and cold by lunch time.

We have talked endlessly about what we should do, particularly about leaving our house. If we had certainty about the future events it would be easier but all we can do is imagine a selection of scenarios depending largely on how long Mother will last. It's rather gruesome. We imagine we will be absent from home for a year, or two at the most. Is that long enough to rent out our house because it certainly can't be left empty in the city; I don't think I want to deal with squatters or vandalism when I get back. But what if she lives for several years? Will we lose touch with our networks, will we even feel a connection to our house when other people have occupied it? Also we would have to let it unfurnished as I couldn't tolerate returning to it if a stranger had been sleeping in my bed, using the belongings that are familiar and often precious to me. My goods and chattels would have to come with us.

The only advantage of renting is an economic one. I have worked out the maths and we would be able to come back with a tidy sum. If Mother went on beyond a couple of years we might even be able to fulfil our pipe dream of retiring to a quiet village in the Peak District or the Lakes.

It is a quantum leap; I really don't know what it might entail for my personal future, what might be demanded of me and whether I would be able to come up to scratch. I have always felt defined by my work, probably to the disadvantage of other relationships; I am a theatre practitioner of several parts, an actor, a Jazz singer, a director, a writer, that is who I am. I have played the part of a nurse on television with some success, but could I ever really be one?

I think perhaps that because she is my Mother the tasks of being her carer should come naturally, in the way that faced with parenthood, even with a complete lack of training, one seems to muddle through with reasonable success. Ah, but there is a significant difference. With parenthood you start with a clean slate, a totally dependant baby who has no knowledge of relationship, no history with you except the gurgles and murmurings she hears from her cosy womb. Also a baby can't talk and therefore can't criticize you; I fear that Mother might. Mother and I have a long established story together, a status established at my birth when apparently I arrived unexpectedly and was almost delivered head first into a handy bucket. Since then I believe I have behaved in a more considerate manner and we have developed a well understood and practised way of relating to each other. Will this all be challenged? Will it all be re-configured? Will I find the challenges intolerable? Will she?

Sometimes moving is a downright stupid idea likely to cause anxiety and regret, but there is something else, something very strong, hard to define. It might be love or loyalty or gratitude or even my stupidly well developed sense of responsibility. You see, I consider my relationship with my Mother to be special, yes, I'm sure many other daughters feel the same, and there are other daughters of my age who may know what I mean and I have met some of them. They are the daughters of war widows. My Mother and my father by all accounts were very much in love, thrown together by the war; she seconded to a teaching post on the East coast and he stationed at a nearby camp. They had such dreams for after the war; settling in the small town where they met, buying a greengrocer shop, a family of five children, membership of the badminton club, frequent visits to London to visit Mother's family, a life full of generosity and love.

I came along when Mother was all alone and father fighting on the front in Europe and naturally I was the apple of their eye and the beginning of the promises they had made to each other. But the dream was killed with him in a foreign land so all she had left was me. The dream was made for three and then we were two, just Mother and me. In the first six or seven years of my life we developed a loyalty to each other, because each other was what we had, and whatever happened in those years has never gone away. We both feel it. I feel it now.

It is odd the way you love somebody you didn't even really know. I feel some kind of affinity with my father and I think some of me is like some of him. I think I do have some snatches of memory; playing tents under the bedclothes with him, the smell of Brylcreem, the scratchiness of his uniform, screeching with pleasure as I was thrown up in the air and caught again, in my Mother's arms waving goodbye to a troop train on the station at dusk with the brown uniformed soldiers leaning out of the windows and the yellow gas lamps flickering. I can recreate all of it with my senses, but what is genuine memory and what is hearsay is blurred. Of course I was fed with wartime propaganda as a very young child and so my father was a giant of a man to me, patriotic, brave, loyal, our country's saviour and, particularly after being killed in action, a hero.

Friends and neighbours would stop in the street to express their condolences to Mother and say how lucky she was to have me, then they would lean down to me to tell me what a hero my father was and how proud I should be as his daughter. I was the consolation prize and I loved it, I felt responsible in my role and it bonded us even closer. However, the enormity of my father's heroic deeds gave me bad dreams. After the war they built a war memorial in the high street with a modest obelisk in the centre surrounded by four square flower beds filled with wallflowers. I used to dream that my father, clad in his army uniform, cap on the side of his head and with his shiny black boots, rose out of the beds, rose to eight feet tall or more and as he hovered there I woke with a start feeling terrified.

9

The sudden entry of Max into our bonded life was shocking. I was told I was going to have a new daddy and the sound of those words are etched into my memory still. I could think of no reason why I should need a new daddy and I hated Max. Max the Usurper. Max the Pretender. I was frequently overcome with rage and jealousy in the early years of their marriage, I resented his presence. Unfortunately for me I can almost relive, after seven decades, the emotion I felt when I saw him kiss my Mother the first time. Because I had hurt my leg I was sitting on our Utility chair that opened out into a bed and they were sitting opposite, both in the same arm chair which confused me enough, but then they kissed and I felt my whole body freeze, my face burn and my tongue gradually push through my lips to point at him in the most insulting gesture I knew. I felt so wicked, I felt so guilty, but somehow I could not help what was happening to me, I could not stop it. There was a horrible silence and then they started shouting. They were angry with me. I didn't understand. Then my Mother, my dear Mother, got up and slapped my leg. I was overwhelmed by the emotions that were wracking my body and I did not understand any of it.

I got more angry as the time passed and there were more occasions to hate him. He once told me not to read in a bad light and an angry bonfire lit in my chest. He wasn't supposed to tell me what to do. He wasn't my daddy. He fitted new handles to a chest of drawers and told me not to tell Mother as it was a surprise and I fell into the childhood joke of saying to Mother that I wasn't allowed to tell her he put new handles on, for which I received another slap from him. I studied the red mark left on my leg and seethed with hatred. He wasn't my daddy. I resented everything he did and said. I thought of ways to kill him. He didn't belong in our life. I was desperately unhappy and felt I had lost any agency with my Mother and in our domestic arrangements.

I'm not sure now how I managed to adapt to Max but I think for most of my Junior School days we jogged along with only minor incidents. Mother bore Max's children and continued her teaching job between them and I was a confused witness to arguments about money and lack of commitment and Max's flirtations with other women. I tolerated him rather than felt any affection and my understanding of the family dynamic was that Mother and I were the couple and Max and his children were an add-on. The climactic event of these years came at Christmas, as these events so often do, and it happened during and because of the Queen's Speech on the wireless.

Max was not pleasant after a drink and he had spent most of the morning in The Swan, returning late while the Christmas dinner was being kept warm for him and we children, now numbering four, were waiting and getting grumpy. He arrived when we were sitting round the dining table laden with the giant turkey, sausages, bread pudding, sprouts and carrots, Yorkshire puddings, roast and mashed potatoes, cranberry jelly and gravy boats. Mother had already carved and was setting out the portions and by the time the Queen began to speak Mother and Max were at each end of the table ready to begin eating the feast. It was the custom, well, Max's custom, that the speech should be heard in silence, it was irreverent to speak while our sovereign was speaking and so the excited chatter from the younger children had been stopped as soon as her Majesty was solemnly announced.

A minute or two in, however, one of the younger children forgot and asked whether he could have some gravy on his potatoes. Max leapt from his chair yelling angrily at the offender who screamed in surprise and fear and Mother intervened in an attempt to calm them both down. Within seconds it was pandemonium with Max yelling and swearing, the offender screaming, Mother shouting at Max, and all the other children crying. The only person who remained calm throughout was the Queen, who soldiered on as if this hideous scene was not happening.

Unfortunately things took a turn for the worse when Max, unable to justify his temper and unable to hear a word the Queen was saying, turned red with rage and took hold of the table from the end where he was sitting and lifted it into the air. During the very short silence that immediately followed, all that could be heard was the Queen and the sound of plates, cutlery, turkey, Yorkshire puddings, gravy boats and every other delight the table had supported sliding down and down and landing in the laps of the children sitting at the low end of the now upended table. When the noise of howling and yelling returned it was deafening.

11

Mother was standing by the door and Max rushed at her, kicking over a chair as he went, and started pummelling her with his fists. Two of the children had run to me, terrified, and were clinging onto my legs and I was screaming at Max to leave Mother alone but he was deaf and blind with rage and stopped only in his own time and he rushed upstairs and was heard swearing and banging about. After only a minute the sorry little group of huddled, weeping children heard the front door slam and it was over.

Of course Mother kept silent, as did the doctor who treated her bruises and broken rib. That is how it was in those days. But I stole the big iron poker we had in the fireplace and kept it under my bed, because I was going to kill Max as soon as he returned home.

I doubt whether Max or Mother really knew how I felt and certainly when Max's children with my Mother came along Max, to his credit, never treated me differently from them. And now he's gone, he died ten years ago, so all that is over, all that is a story now. Mother didn't have an easy time with him but she amused me so much at Max's grave after his funeral. I think on these occasions you are supposed to say loving words over the grave but she leant over to it and said 'I'm sorry I nagged you so much, but you deserved it.'

***

I have never thought of my childhood as difficult or harmful but it certainly wasn't uneventful and some of the things that happened might have contributed to attitudes and emotions I experience now. I remember mostly the sunny happy days and am merely curious about the potentially damaging ones. I have had a very untidy life, adapting and re-adapting to changing circumstances, but always surviving, even if it is by the skin of my teeth. The unconditional and undying love from my Mother, the safety blanket she held out to me even when I was an adult, has always held me from falling too badly. But I am not so good at meeting change these days, I have lost some of the confidence of my early years, my tread on uneven ground is not so steady.

There is no doubt about it, radical change is harder when you get older; I am sixty nine next birthday, after which I will be in my seventieth year. I have got old and I never thought it would happen to me. I have lived in so many houses, moved all over the country chasing the work, I have taken Mother and Max on foreign holidays and in my fifties I arranged band tours for demanding musicians as far away as New Orleans. Now I am quaking at the thought of packing up my home and moving to a place which is already very familiar to me. But I am the only one who, in practical terms, can up sticks and go to care for Mother. I am the only family member with the flexibility to do it, having left behind the necessity to earn by claiming my senior citizen's pension and turning work into an occasional delight. The two opposing arguments, to stay or to leave, are drawing together to close the gap ready for the decision, but it is going to be a hard one and it must be made soon.

Chapter Two

METAMORPHOSIS

I am sitting alone in the attic of my Mother's house which has now become our bedroom and I am crying. I don't know whether it is from anger, frustration, pity, self-pity, regret, guilt, or all of those things. Anyway, I'm sitting on my mattress which is on the floor because the base of my bed wouldn't go up the attic stairs and is now getting mouldy, along with other beloved items of our furniture, in a damp storage unit. This is merely one of the reasons for my emotional turmoil.

In order to make this room habitable I have had to sort through years and years of 'stored' items banished to the attic by the family as a default space when decisions about their future could not be negotiated. I have already got rid of the two beds that were kept up here for visitors; they have gone to the tip as they would have been no use to anyone since moths have eaten numerous holes in the mattresses. I wonder if any of the visitors knew that a sheet's distance away from their slumbering forms, little moth maggots were hatching and beginning to nibble their way into the world.

The destination for some of the stuff was obvious and bin bags began to fill with old wallpaper and Christmas wrapping, fragile and nibbled by creatures unknown, broken lamps, and books unopened for thirty years that filled the air with paper dust. No wonder my grandson developed an allergic reaction whenever he came to stay with great grannie and slept up here in the attic! With every bag delivered down the two flights of stairs Mother would wait until I had gone back up and then rifle through them to check what I had thrown away. I could, with some irritation, hear the rustling and grumbling although I don't think she found a single item that was retrievable. Just as well because once that trust had been broken it

14

would be very hard to restore it; I would have been more closely monitored at every step.

Despite the absence of the huge haul of inspected rubbish, the attic room is cramped with an odd assortment of our furniture; cupboards from different rooms in our old house now piled on top of each other, touching the low ceiling, Joe's computer desk stuffed at the foot of his bed with barely room to sit in his chair, bin bags full of our belongings piled ceiling high in corners and nowhere to hang our clothes. There is only just enough room to squeeze between it all to move about the room. Getting dressed and undressed is a balancing act in a foot wide space beside the bed, but at least you can't loose your socks under the bed, there isn't room for them. The only pleasurable space in the room is through the window which affords a sylvan vista of spacious green fields dotted with sheep.

***

I've heard jokes about how inflexible elderly people can be but now I meet the reality head on. Mother doesn't like any changes that I try to make and has got quite aggressive about a modest cat scratching post I put in the sitting room intending to divert feline attention from her furniture. Once when I wasn't there she made Joe put my vintage stool in the leaky shed and she doesn't see why I want a full size cutting board to prepare food on when she has managed with the broken half of a bread board all these years. Her rather strident objection to the cat scratching post was that she 'didn't want to look it' and she put up the same phrase one rainy day when I placed the airer laden with wet washing indoors. How else was I to get the sheets dry?

Her breakfast requirements are precise; two prunes, three dried apricots, one slice tinned grapefruit and once slice of toast thinly spread with butter followed by a medley of prescribed drugs with coffee. Any variation to absolutely anything requires an explanation and probably an argument.

The shower days are Sunday, Wednesday and Friday. After lunch at two o'clock she goes to bed for a rest; I like this bit because sometimes I need a lie down too, and she is woken with a cup of tea ready to go down to the sitting room. The television goes on at five

15

o'clock when she watches a quiz programme that defies understanding. However baffling the content, she is always pleased when someone wins the jackpot. The quiz is followed by the national and local news and whatever she can find on BBC one or two, venturing into other channels is not deemed appropriate or necessary, and the television goes off at nine o'clock. Essential programs are Gardener's World and Countryfile but she is also partial to wildlife documentaries and will happily sit of an evening watching wild animals copulating and tearing each other to pieces.

Having realised that if we shared a sitting room with Mother, Joe and I would be expected to tolerate all her television programmes and have no privacy unless we were in bed in the miserable attic, we made an early decision to have our own sitting room in the 'Master Bedroom' and to move Mother into the smaller bedroom. It also alleviated the worry of her crossing the top of stairs at night on her frequent trips to the bathroom; she would be on the same level as the bathroom and next door to it.

Actually this is one change that she really appreciates. The 'Master Bedroom' is big enough for a double bed, chest of drawers, large wardrobe and so on, all the usual bedroom things, but it has a tiny window looking out on a wall across a narrow road and facing almost North so there is very little light or warmth, making it feel dark and dismal. The small bedroom is only big enough for a single bed, wardrobe, chest of drawers and bed side table, but it faces South with a picture window overlooking the garden and hill beyond, which makes the ambience much more significant than the lack of space.

I have painted her new bedroom moss green, put up pretty new curtains, had a new carpet fitted and bought her a new single bed from Argos with duvet covers that co-ordinate with the rest of the room. Pictures have been hung, ornaments arranged and she has moved in.

She absolutely loves it. She finds it calming and peaceful and can watch from her bed the cattle and the deer that roam the hill. She wishes she had thought of it before. She calls it her 'little nest'. It has been one of the more successful interventions I have made in order to enlarge the household from one person to three persons and four cats and for all of us to remain moderately sane.

16

Madge called the other day and Mother insisted she go upstairs to admire the new bedroom. I could tell that Madge was reluctant but Mother insisted and as I followed her up I could see why. Madge was so wobbly on the stairs and yet she had refused to use the chair lift. Some time ago Madge fell in her garden and was lying on the ground for two hours before Leo came back from his walk to find her. She had broken her leg and had gone through the expected painful recovery, but if you asked her about it you would think by her reaction she had suffered an insignificant graze. There is something extraordinary about this generation of women and the way they minimise difficulty. Anyway Madge was suitably impressed with the bedroom and fascinated by the view of the hill which is seen from a unique angle from this house making it remarkably different from Madge's house next door but one.

We are almost done with projects within our own capabilities and these have been accomplished with only moderate objections and have even received a modicum of gratitude once completed. We have changed a kitchen carpet suspected of harbouring wildlife for tile effect, hygienic cushion floor, have put lights in a walk in cupboard and oiled hinges on windows and gates that wouldn't either open or close. We're getting there.

***

The most expensive project was in many ways the most important simply because it was an urgent matter to protect our health and safety. The first alarm came when my daughter, who was visiting on one of the occasions that Mother was in hospital, was helping me to cook the dinner. Without warning there was a loud explosion from the electric cooker and all the electrics in the house went off. We were stunned, not physically, but with astonishment and wonder at what we had done to cause such an alarming reaction. The only thing left working was the old fashioned phone which still had the emergency red button installed from when Mother was living alone. Amidst the ensuing chaos someone called from the red button to see if everything was all right.

This was totally beyond our limited skills base so we called Charlie, the local electrician, who came at once. He diagnosed the fault in the connection of the cooker to the mains in the wall, saying it was 'an accident waiting to happen' as the cooker had been connected without the earth and who on earth had done the work.

Well of course it was Max, who considered himself a dab hand at almost everything and who for the past forty years had re-jigged, re-modelled, re-wired, re-painted, re-plumbed and re-built most of the house and its fixtures and fittings. Max's creative programme was not usually supported by maintenance, but he and Mother had bumbled along nicely enough with Max's improvisations. Mother was not inclined to blame Max about the cooker, considering that nothing had happened before, and instead theorised that the cooker had blown up because I carried a lot of static and therefore it was my fault.

I believe Mother had purposely never learnt about electricity, mechanics or anything remotely technical. Perhaps that was why she never learnt to drive. But it did mean she could avoid a lot of household jobs and since Max was willing to take them on, regardless of expertise, that suited her at the time. She once advised her three daughters to learn to say 'I can't' more often, as the omission of it would lead to them having to do 'everything' without help.

We asked Charlie to carry out a general survey of the electrics and he came up with a number of problems and several additional 'accidents waiting to happen'. The thermostats in the storage heaters didn't work properly, nor did the one in the hot water tank. There was an overload on the landing which caused the lights to shut off as a safety measure thus plunging Mother into darkness on her way to her nocturnal wee and inadvertently causing another hazard. There was no light on the attic stairs, the bathroom heater had been left on long enough to melt the plastic casing, there were very few sockets meaning overuse of trailing leads, the microwave was apparently dangerous and then his two favourites; a socket stuck to the wallpaper with glue and the wires of a lamp cable joined to the wires of another cable by ancient, browning sellotape.

Credit must be given where it is due; Max's willingness to attempt DIY alterations was in many ways admirable and did display quite a range of skills. Max was one of those people blessed with talents in mind and body; his intellect had benefited from a good private education and he was widely read but he could also turn his hand to practical tasks and many of his projects were successful and even stood the test of time. I can understand why the house had suffered from neglect as the two of them got older; lack of mobility and strength confined them, lack of energy depleted them and those who only visited may not have noticed some of the conditions that we, as residents, were alarmed by.

Negotiating these changes was not at all easy. Mother stuck to her premise that since she had managed all these years there was no need for change, particularly if it cost money, and although the changes were in some ways quite small and unobtrusive she became agitated at each one. Sometimes she will get tearful, sometimes angry at what she considers are my unnecessary arrangements. Sometimes she argues in a sulky way, at others she cries like an unjustly punished child, a baby, and accuses me of 'always telling her off.' Her reaction seems unreasonable and often out of proportion and it is extremely hurtful. I feel embarrassed at her childish behaviour, that my Mother whom I have admired and respected has demeaned herself by adopting this low status as the victim and cast me as an aggressor. I want to love my Mother as I have always done but at these times I find it too difficult.

I do wonder how different it might have been if Mother had been able to move into our house, whether she would have appreciated that we had our own lives, our own community, our own interests and therefore our own value. She might have realised that we were giving up part of our lives to benefit her, whereas now she doesn't see that we have actually left behind almost every piece of our lives to look after her. Instead we have moved into her rigid life and have been obliged to alter it. Perhaps it is easier if the person who needs care leaves their old life and their old habits behind and in order to be safe they are obliged to adapt to their hosts' home and lifestyle. I don't think she has tried to understand all this; she is tuned in to thinking that everyone wants to live down here in the country, that it is some kind of blessing, and why on earth would they prefer the city.

Thinking back to her past history since she moved to Cornwall there have been numerous people who have used her and her little house for holidays and even used it as a half way house before moving here to settle in their own homes. So I think she might even see it as giving us a wonderful opportunity. But Joe and I have discussed whether we might want to retire to Cornwall and we have rejected the idea; we like the north and we know it has every advantage, both town and country, to offer.

Those emotions that I have mentioned earlier, anger, frustration, pity, regret, guilt, are present in one form or another almost every day and for the first time for many years I have sometimes felt I would rather not be here. I mean here, in this world, alive. Sometimes I desperately want to run away but I have nowhere to run to. I am trapped. I have trapped myself. But what can you do when these oppressive thoughts won't keep away, thoughts and feelings that are generated by an external force rather than a crossed wire in my own mind? Six weeks counselling is not going to alter this situation I have brought upon myself and my husband. Six hours of talking to a stranger will not reveal any more than I already am aware of myself. It would be more therapeutic to talk to my cats, which I already do with increasing frequency.

So I sit in the attic and love my cat, who doesn't mind if I cry as long as she gets cuddles and food and who won't tell anyone what I have told her or think badly of me for it. And before my absence is noticed and explanations are asked for I must go downstairs and carry on. My next job, which will probably give rise to protestations of innocence, is to clear out a cupboard in the kitchen which contains strong and dangerous medicines that were prescribed for Max who died ten years ago. Perhaps I will wait until Mother is asleep!

***

Mother has been through a predictable and yet unexpected metamorphosis; unfortunately not the usual kind that turns the ugly grub into the exquisite butterfly, but possibly quite the reverse. Unexpected because like many of us she has procrastinated facing the truth of old age and she has lived for so long that she has ended up a person out of place in time, She lives in a century she does not belong in and hardly understands.

Everyone knows, indeed it is a well rehearsed joke amongst the middle aged who notice their first grey hair or dodgy knee, everyone knows that the one thing in life you can't stop is ageing. You can dye your hair, update your wardrobe, go to pilates or play the on-trend boy band on your car stereo with the window open, but you're still going to get old. Sorry, it's true.

I started off wanting to be older, this was when I was six, and I thought it would be wonderful to be seven, it sounded like a really good age, so grown up. Then I realised that I was in fact in my seventh year and, although I had not completed it yet, I felt I was justified in calling myself seven. Having found I could manipulate time in this way I vowed that seven was my lucky number and I still use it for my lottery tickets. Unfortunately it has not yet reached its potential.

So age is only a matter of perception and is only numbers anyway, until things start to break. The body is not as imaginative as the mind and despite the mind's efforts to influence the body's feeble responses to ageing, the body usually wins. My most startling realisation of where I was in my life span came at about fifty when I suddenly realised that I hadn't got enough time left to read all the books I wanted to read or listen to all the music I had intended to. If, or when, that happens there is so much left to do that you don't know where to start anyway.

When I was in my early twenties, and still in the bloom of youth as it were, I was once sitting in my theatre dressing room with other actors talking about age. It was a particularly relevant conversation in those days of repertory theatre as actors were employed as a company for a long season and the same actors played in every play, which meant in one week you might be playing the sprightly young juvenile lead and the next week the aged dowager. I think I played more elderly women in my twenties than I ever played when I actually looked the part and then spent my fiftieth birthday on a film set playing the Mother of seven year old twins; I didn't dare tell the cast and crew it was my birthday in case they asked which one. In those early days of my life attempting to represent fictional women I thought I understood the transformations of old age; the slowing of

21

metabolism, the change of rhythms, the fragility of movement, and found I had a fond fascination for those elderly characters of my youth. Now I know what it's really like to have a dodgy knee and get breathless on a hill I realise it is much more fun to act it.

I recognise many of the same genes in myself as in my Mother and sometimes it is like watching an instructional film showing myself in years to come, although in reality she puts to shame my feeble efforts to keep going. She too has led an active life, pushing into the distance the whole idea of incapacity whilst raising six children, working full time, contributing to the community, engaging in sporting activity and, even in her eighties, striding along the cliff paths in all weathers. It has been a life full of action and heavy responsibilities, in charge of children, groups of people and decision making. It is very hard to let it go even when her only action is to struggle from chair to wheelchair, her only decision to suggest which ready meal might be nice for tea. She still defines herself as a woman capable and experienced and able to shoulder responsibility and it is these very experiences that developed her strength of spirit which she now calls to battle in an attempt to preserve them. But as each facility weakens and declines it is replaced by frustration and loss of self.

Now I sometimes see the small signposts to my own transformation; that slow, inevitable decline in my own mobility, the extraordinary realisation that I can no longer hop in any remotely dignified manner or kneel down without groaning. I really do wonder sometimes whether I am going to be up to this job physically and I already know that mentally it's going to be challenging. Of course this is the dilemma that my generation now face, probably the first generation to do so in such numbers, that our parents are now living so long that they need a carer when their sons, and particularly their daughters, are observing the first stages of their own decline as they enter their third age.

I am beginning to understand why so many parents of disabled children find their relationship so difficult to maintain and sometimes need to separate. Of course I couldn't possibly fully understand; my situation is quite different, but I feel the gradual subjugation of my life to the essentials of my caring role and with it the diminishing of social networks and the difficulty of giving time to other relationships.

***

I've just read an essay on being a carer for the elderly. I'm pretty sure the writer has never been one, or else they were writing for an audience who didn't want an accurate response to the experience. Perhaps it was advertising copy for a carer's recruitment agency or perhaps the writer was laying a smooth surface on her path to heaven. Certainly there is love that is almost unconditional although it is very hard to lay down any of your own conditions given the elderly person's needs. As a carer you are committed to do whatever your subject needs and not necessarily what you need and possibly the two needs will seldom coincide.

Of course there may be a thinly hidden agenda in some people's motivation which energises them when they care for elderly relatives with one eye on the will. Well, that's what you see in the movies and art and reality do have a very close relationship. I have heard of a couple that did target elderly people in the guise of the good Samaritan and found they could collect the cash as easily as taking honey from the bees.

Even a deep love and respect for the person you are caring for will not make all the essential tasks pleasant, it will not prevent you from getting exhausted, it will not prevent you from getting angry and frustrated when you meet the kind of obstinate, ungrateful, demanding or critical behaviour an elderly person is prone to deliver.

I don't know whether I can expect Mother's attitudes to change so perhaps it is up to me to work around them but I am afraid of what it might do to me and to my relationship with Joe if I am constantly subduing my feelings. There is an underlying tension present most of the time and I have already had arguments with Joe and been what previously I might have called rude to Mother but which was about defining necessary boundaries.

I don't want to go on feeling that I am merely a surrogate for her legs and arms, for her disability to carry out daily tasks. It dehumanises me. Joe and I need to feel we are not only here for Mother's benefit but we also have to live our lives, to develop and

23

grow and find our own place in this new community. I am torn between Mother and Joe; I am beginning to loose who I am. I even said last week that I would go back home if she didn't stop complaining; I regret saying it now, it was said in anger. Later she asked me if I was happy and my answer stuck in my throat, I just couldn't say 'yes' so I mumbled something about being all right, which I clearly wasn't.

***

Today I'm looking back on last week and thinking maybe it was some kind of turning point. Maybe the tension had reached breaking point, probably when I said I might go home, because things feel a little different this week. Mother has asked me if I would like an area of the garden to call my own, where I could decide what to grow, perhaps grow some vegetables. Actually I don't want this because the garden is so very much hers; I don't think I could alter anything without causing her to feel regretful about it. Imagine pulling up some plant she has nurtured for forty years and dumping it in the compost bin. No, I couldn't, although I do realise she is willing to sacrifice something she loves to make me feel happy. She also suggested that Joe and I could go out together regularly while she is having her afternoon rest and this is a welcome suggestion, I would really like to go out just for a bag of chips and a beer once a week which we could easily do while she sleeps.

So I think she is emerging from a necessarily selfish place, which perhaps a person who has lived and survived alone for some time, ordering their own lives, making their own rules, needs to create for their own preservation and she is ready to embrace the idea that the household is now the three of us, plus cats, and we all need to make a life together. I would dearly like to respond to this positively and encourage a new dynamic amongst us that we can all live with.

Chapter Three

MOTHER'S AMAZING GARDEN

Well that's my gardening over for today. I watch the drip drip of blood from my finger to the white bathroom basin, its wiggly path until it meets the wet ceramic and then its burgeoning into a multi faceted star shape and the fading of the blood red into pink. It's a lot of blood for what is only a small cut.

It has been a lovely Spring day with warm sunshine and all three of us have been working in the garden all afternoon with that particular energy that comes with the first signs of life returning after the Winter. Mother went inside first having had a good dose of fresh air and Joe went to make a cup of tea and I stayed behind to clear up. Unfortunately one of the pieces of blue and white china which emerge at intervals from the soil managed to slice into my finger. Such a shame that the day should end with me running to the house holding up my bleeding finger.

Downstairs Joe is having a frantic exchange with Mother as she tries to command the situation from her arm chair. 'Where do you keep the plasters?' he asks. 'In the cupboard where they've always been.' Mother replies, somewhat tersely considering the possible medical emergency and the fact that Joe has not 'always been' in this house.

'They're not here.'

'Yes they are.'

I wrap my finger in a blue flannel and hold it as I go to the top of the stairs ready to referee the developing confrontation. He finds the plasters before I have a chance to shout and bounds up the stairs holding them out to me.

Well you know how difficult it is to put a plaster on with one hand, so we struggle together to even get the plasters out of the cardboard box. They are all stuck together and when we manage to separate one and tear off the outer cover we find a old, discoloured, thick pinky beige fabric rectangle with sticky glue oozing from the sides. We eventually decide that the inner pad has a fifty fifty chance of remaining sterile and is better than the blue flannel and the bleeding is staunched.

Drama over, I ask Mother how long she has had the plasters. It's hard to believe her assurances when I notice the price on the cardboard box; these are antique plasters.

***

The garden is, possibly, but only possibly, after her children, the most important part of Mother's life. She describes it as 'forty years of hard work' and she declares her love of it frequently. I will have to describe the then and now pictures of the garden briefly for you to become familiar with it as a setting for my Mother's love.

As I look out on it now and step from the back door it begins with a large stone paved patio the width of the house. The patio is almost covered in pots filled with a smorgasbord of colourful flowers and against the house wall is a huge passion flower to one side of the door and a clematis to the other. There used to be a wisteria there, but the house being tiny and the wisteria huge and vigorous they had to cut it down before it devoured the whole house. As it is, the roots of the current resident flora are beginning to borrow under the walls, something I will have to employ some diplomacy to deal with. Removing a plant is like removing one of Mother's friends.

Below the patio are two stone terraces forming a mezzanine level and to the left some ancient steps curve down through a rose arch to the third level of the garden which runs in a horizontal plane for a dozen yards through lawn, borders and rose beds. An old stone path leads down its length to a rough timber bridge over a fast flowing stream which is home for eels and voles and then to the bluebell filled bank beyond and the boundary of Mother's property. Then, lastly, the land rises steeply again through two fields of pasture and ends at the horizon lined neatly with distant overgrown hedges, May and Hawthorn, with blossom in Spring and red berries in Autumn. Despite the pasture being owned by the farm and overlooked by several neighbouring houses, Mother considers this to be her own hill, and on her hill graze bullocks and deer and she can watch out for the occasional rabbit or fox. The lawn I mentioned is merely a token backdrop for the borders and beds which are stuffed full with shrubs and flowers and spring bulbs. It is a riot of planting, a prodigious abundance.

Moving to this tiny house, in this county, was a result of a love affair with Cornwall following many family holidays, the family then consisting of herself, Max and their two youngest children. Even this morning I looked again in wonder at a photograph of the 'before' garden and still can't imagine what drew her to the house. Imagine the land that greeted her; a builder's yard of dead, dusty soil full of gravel, broken glass and broken concrete. Where the stone terraces now stand, a sloping mess of tumbling rubble down to the level wilderness where nettles, bindweed and goose grass ran through brambles in a joyous riot. Beyond the stream a bank, now filled with bluebells and nodding daffodils, but which was for decades, if not centuries, used as a dumping ground for rubbish from the families now decaying in the village graveyard, whose discarded clay pipes, ridged medicine bottles and cracked bowls surface now and then to confirm the garden's rich history.

***

This is the third garden Mother has created. Mother and I started out during the war in various 'digs' and in peace time settled in the ground floor flat of a large house with an un-gardened garden of gravel and weeds at the back shared with the upstairs occupant. Strange to think of it nowadays but the upstairs access was outside by means of a long iron staircase and the Mr. Rowney who lived there had only one leg, the other being lost in a war. From downstairs I could hear him painstakingly clumping up the ringing iron steps one by one, real leg first then heaving up his false leg. I think the war where he left his leg must have been in India because in his flat were statues and ornaments of tigers and elephants. He once showed me his false leg, smooth and brown and un-leglike, and the image is still held in my mind's eye to this day. The rest of Mr. Rowney was unmemorable in the light of his most astonishing feature. I was fascinated by the strange leg and not at all curious about or frightened by any trauma he might have felt as he lost his real one. I do wonder now whether the leg was made of Bakelite because our old wireless was made of a similar material and these were pre-plastic days.

I visited Mr. Rowney upstairs often and was allowed to take his mysterious objects out of the glass cabinets and hold them. They smelt of something far away, of a hot, musty land that was nothing like England. Sometimes he would take me for a ride on his invalid carriage, sitting on his lap and holding the handlebars with him and once he took me to the Golf Club and I saw a snake swimming in a pond. I didn't like or dislike Mr. Rowney. I liked his flat and what was in it and I liked riding in the invalid chair and I liked the fact that he had a false leg. But apparently he liked me and when he asked Mother if he could adopt me and educate me at an exclusive and extremely expensive private school, my visits to the upstairs flat were abruptly stopped.

There were only two notable incidents in this garden; one was the great East coast flood when my new brother was found asleep in his Silver Cross pram floating around the garden, the other was after Max had told me that cats always land on their feet and I carried the black kitten I was given for my fifth birthday up the iron staircase and dropped it over the edge and was severely punished for simply researching the hypothesis. Incidentally, they do land on their feet – hypothesis verified and kitten surprised but not harmed.

Mother's next garden was where I spent my childhood from age eight to leaving home for drama school. It was a long, thin one, the width of the semi-detached house she shared with Max and their first-born son and me, my kitten and a dog. There were two ramshackle sheds full of spiders at the bottom, a mature apple tree, a Worcester Pearmain, and rough grass. Over the years the garden changed as more children were born and Mother got caught up in the hurly burly of a large family, peppered with a teaching job and occasionally time for her hobby as an amateur actress. But it was always coloured with flowers and we children played happily in it through the changing of the seasons and we ate our apples, and next door's pears, and gooseberries and currants that Mother had planted and dug holes towards Australia. Mother allowed us our freedom amongst her flowers in a most generous way and we peopled the garden with guinea pigs, cats and dogs, doves and terrapins, rabbits, cricket stumps painted on the wall and crabs in buckets in the outside loo.

Later, long after I left home, Mother and Max and my half-siblings, now mostly adolescents, moved to a four bedroom detached surrounded by large gardens. This is where Mother came into her own as a horticulturist and created a garden that did not need to accommodate anything but her own imagination and hard work, followed, of course, by her enjoyment. It was an ordered, designed garden but still with her hallmark of profusion planting

***

Now, of course, she can't manage the garden, it is even difficult for her to get down the steps, even with help, onto the level area of lawn. She can just about manage to get around with a stick, and this last bit of mobility allows her to water the garden, every evening, rain or shine. With a hose fitted to an outdoor tap and the water switched to its full force she can stand in one place in the middle of the patio clinging onto a chair and bombard the pots and troughs and climbing plants that surround her. Then, by clinging onto one garden chair after another, she can take an unsteady route through the pools of water to the patio edge, where she points the hose nozzle skywards creating a sparkling arc of water to reach the plants at the bottom of the mezzanine terraces.

She pays no attention to the fact that the water is metered and her bill is enormous and to keep myself calm about this I equate her water usage to a leisure activity, such as membership of a golf club, where the fees might very well surpass the amounts she has paid to the water company. It is interesting that water did not seem to be rationed during the war and I wonder if her lifelong love of unconstrained freedom of its use might be a throwback to those times. Now of course we have a reversal of the assumption that water is free and in endless supply and understand that every resource the planet provides must be nurtured.

I am not currently required to do much of the heavy gardening because she has help in the form of Drew. Drew arrives every Thursday and stands in the kitchen waiting for today's orders.

Having received and understood, he picks his way down the garden to start work. I say 'picks' because Drew can never pass a weed without uprooting it, so the weeds he spots dictate his path and he meanders to their tune. It is often difficult to find Drew in the garden because he blends into it; he wears an oversized camouflage jacket and a hat adorned with feathers and sprouting from the hat is bushy brown hair and a bushy brown beard with two black sparkling eyes and a beaky sort of nose. I would say he is probably in excess of fifty years younger than Mother, certainly two generations distant, and their relationship reminds me of the film 'Driving Miss Daisy' in which two totally different people of totally different cultures and generations find a way to chug along despite their difference. If Mother saw Drew out of context she would probably be most disapproving and would certainly not have given him house room.

In fine weather Mother likes to 'sit out' on the patio; in cool weather with a blanket round her knees and, in the heat ,with a linen garden hat and parasol. She watches and counts. She counts everything, and the higher the numbers the better, unless it is slugs in which case the lower the better. Her favourite subjects for a count are roses and she will be able to tell any visitor to the house how many are on each of the many bushes she has planted and nurtured over the years and compare that with the count of the previous year. Bulbs take over from roses in the Spring. Second favourite subjects for a count are the bullocks, often up to thirty, who saunter across the field from East to West each day, sometimes pausing to flop down together to take a rest from their leisurely progress. A special treat are the fallow deer, usually five, who venture out of the little copses that line the hill and nuzzle their way through the grasses and low branches or run and leap at speed across the slopes.

Unseen and therefore uncounted in the usual run of things are the animals underground. No, I don't mean worms and beetles who are too numerous to count anyway, I am talking about the dead pets. In size they range from a Doberman to a hamster and although I know that Tibbs the cat is under the bird bath and Blair the dog is under the round rose bed, the whereabouts of many are uncertain and digging in the garden is always cautious and not too deep.

Design in the garden is not as important to Mother as quantity and this is rather obvious when I take her to the garden centre. Her modus operandi is to grab whatever might suddenly take her fancy, regardless of cost or plan, as I wheel her through the tempting displays. When asked where she is thinking of putting the chosen plant her answer is always that she will 'find somewhere' and as a result the garden is a riot of colour and shape, pleasing in its abundance but not an example that might be featured on Gardener's World as elegant in design. Mother was distressed and angry lately, and quite rightly, when the house was valued and the estate agent's report described the garden as 'overgrown'. The man was a fool and did not appreciate that every flower, leaf and stalk had been chosen and nurtured and constantly loved and valued. It was profusion he could not understand and his glancing view interpreted it as 'neglected'. A written apology was demanded and received but there has always been a trace of anger left, which surfaces whenever visitors comment favourably on Mother's horticultural efforts and the story is retold.

Watching is also an active and even industrious occupation. She can watch from the patio in fine weather or from her chair in the kitchen which faces the glass door to the garden. Mother will always know the direction of the wind because she watches the cloud movements and the swinging of the weather vane with its two dimensional metal owl perched on the arrow. She will also observe the development of each plant and watch expectantly for its next phase. She watches the sparrows as they come and go between their nest in the corner of the roof and the bird table and she watches the blackbirds as they pull worms and beetles from the grass. The visits of the robin, blue tits and finches are a constant delight to her. She loves to make up messy suet balls for her birds but gets angry with the jackdaws for taking too big a share of the goodies she provides. The arrival of a pigeon at the feeding station almost always results in a shaking fist and a stream of barrack room expletives. She is merely protecting the things she loves, as anyone would do. There is nothing about or in the garden that she does not have intimate knowledge of, no part of it that she has not touched or been touched by.

The one horticultural element within her sights which gives her more frustration than pleasure, and one that she has a baffling relationship with, is grass, and the problem she appears to have with it is that it grows. She becomes quite agitated if the lawn grows to

31

mowing height before Thursday, Drew's gardening day. The poor daisies and celandines have adapted well to a mere week's uninhibited growth; I have never seen such short yet fully developed flowers. Nature fighting back!

The field on the hill is of even greater concern. As a field it is naturally prone to clumping grass and an uneven appearance which is partially levelled when there is a large enough herd of bullocks curling their huge tongues round the clumps of fresh grass and munching their way across the field. But if the herd change their routine and favour an alternative route for a few days the effect is noticeable on the growth of grass. When they disappear, probably onto somebody's dinner table, the effect is even more pronounced, especially to Mother who will by now be in a state of anxiety. Madge doesn't help because she too is a counter of bullocks and a watcher of clumping grass and the two of them wind each other up. I have several times had to dissuade these agitated old ladies from phoning the farmer to complain about the appearance of the field.

***

Every gardener knows that with the joys of gardening also come the battles with the flora and fauna of the region. I have already mentioned daisies and celandine of the lawn and clumping grass of the field and the ubiquitous bindweed, nettles and goose grass need no mention at all if you are a gardener, you will know them. But the arch enemy of all horticulture, occupant of first place in every survey in Gardener's World, is the demonic slug. Mother's garden is a haven for the terrestrial gastropod; vertical living is supplied for snails in dense green climbers clinging to the walls, slug nurseries abound in crevices in the old stone garden walls and the scattered clay and plastic flower pots provide social habitats for slugs, worms and woodlice.

Mother's main defence was the twilight hunt armed with a tub of Co-op salt. She would have been an asset to any military force with her determined and vigorous approach to battle. First came the reconnoitre of the whole garden seeking out the enemy and where she found them a swift blast on the weapon would finish them off in a shrinking, squirming, slimy agony. Favourite plants were often treated to a protective circle of glistening crystals and areas of suspicion given a generous arc of the white stuff in the hope that an unwary slug or snail would err across the deadly path. I have never heard salt recommended as a beneficial nutrient for plant growth but Mother's garden is a testament to its possible lack of harm at least.

The joy of the hunt is not possible now. Her balance is too wobbly. Although on one occasion at least she managed to sneak out for a daylight sortie when Joe and I had gone out together on a quick trip to the village and on returning we found she had spread poisonous slug pellets all over the patio. Because she had to support herself with one hand on her stick, the other hand with the tub of pellets in it was rather uncoordinated and all she could was to swing the open tub about, sending pellets in every direction.

We were horrified! The pellets were everywhere that our cats might walk on them, lick their paws and be poisoned. Mother insisted that they were harmless, that she had used them for years with no poison cases, that we were making a fuss. I got hold of the container and showed her where it said they were 'lethal' to pets, that they could 'cause death' and she changed from indignant denials to tearful excuses but couldn't quite make it as far as apologies. It took over an hour to clear up the pellets but I think, well I know, I got every one or I would not have been able to sleep that night.

Another important art of destruction, or in this case it could more reasonably be seen as recycling, that Mother has always relished is the bonfire. A garden like this produces an enormous amount of organic waste and the system is that the soft stuff goes in the compost bin and the twigs and branches are burnt. She loves bonfires! I can see why. Fire is always exciting and the outdoor sights of tall flames dancing up and down against the background of the field, smoke billowing through the branches of nearby trees and sparks flashing and crackling several feet upwards against a darkening sky is magical. It is so satisfying to know that what grew in the garden stays in the garden and the ashes that it makes grow next year's roses.

We got ready for the bonfire this morning. I gathered all the long cuttings from the roses and hazels and flowering current that I had cut back earlier and Mother sat at the table on the patio and cut them into short lengths. She looked so at home in her flowered sun hat

33

with her gardening gloves and secateurs and her usual determined expression snipping away confidently. Just for this moment she wasn't old and disabled and needy in so many ways. She was the Mother I had always known and loved, kind, gentle and self sufficient and a skilled and knowledgeable gardener. I had to stop what I was doing and watch. I felt a strange mixture of extreme sadness and pride and somehow I knew I was looking at a special picture that I would not see for very much longer, that I must treasure this picture, that this was yet another 'last time'.

Unfortunately my reverie was short lived. Once Joe and I got the fire ready for lighting with a good supply of cardboard to keep the slightly damp vegetation going, Mother insisted on coming down the steps to the level of the garden to watch. We knew we were in for trouble but how could we deny her this pleasure? So I helped her down one step at a time with many wobblings and grabbings on the way and managed to get her onto a chair within a safe distance of the fire. Of course Mother is a very experienced bonfire maker, the same is true of the sitting room fire, but Joe and I are quite capable too. The trouble is she just doesn't trust us and every time we have any kind of fire she insists on supervising. So throughout the bonfire she shouts instructions, loudly. 'Poke it, poke it!' she yells 'No not there, the other side! Put that box on! No not that one! Look out! That bit's going to fall! Watch it doesn't catch the tree branch!' and so on and so on until the mound of combustibles is merely smoking red embers. She loved it.

***

Mother has a pre-paid funeral plan, so all her wishes are laid down clearly, including the wording of a notice to be placed in a certain shop window in the village. Several of her wishes are difficult but I don't think I will tell her.

Firstly the shop window she has chosen went out of business years ago and I already know I will feel a pang of guilt if the notice has to go in a different shop. I'm not going to tell her, I bet she has the image of it already imagined. She wants to be cremated and the crematorium is a long distance from here and she wants people to know that she won't mind if they can't make the journey. Typical

34

Mother! So considerate. She wants 'Glad That I Live Am I' sung at the funeral service. I know it and it is a really difficult one to sing with its changing of rhythm, the service could end in a car crash as people try to follow it. I might ask my niece in law, who has a lovely voice, to sing it solo so as not to ruin the pretty song and embarrass the congregation.

The last one is tricky too. She wants her ashes scattered in the garden. Of course this would be entirely appropriate and for her to grow into her plants would be wonderful in some ways. But it worries me. I am afraid I will be weeding or pruning or digging and I will feel her eyes on me and I will hear her voice and know that I have done it all wrong. I might even hear her voice ringing out from the rose beds 'That's not the right way to do it!' She has said, just once, that she might change her mind and request that she is tipped into the stream in the garden so that she can burble along with the eels under the neighbour's little bridges and spread right out when she reaches the sea. I think this is a really good idea but I don't think it would be ethical for me to influence her. I did say the sea choice was good and romantic though.

So today as the last spiral of smoke rose from our bonfire I was clearing up the odd twigs that had got left out and thinking what a good job she didn't notice those, and I began to reminisce about Mother's gardening life and how it may have saved her. These days we know that there is a plethora of drugs that can aid stress and poor mental health; most of us are not afraid to tell a doctor we have a problem of the mind rather than the body. We can even switch on a phone or a computer and get advice and medication from the internet. Mother had nothing like this and yet she did have almost everything that would lead to low level stress or worse; too many children, a demanding job, a difficult husband, financial instability, and yet what she fought any ailment with was a single paracetamol. We now also know that contact with the natural world, grass under the feet, soil under the fingernails, fresh air in the lungs, can be as efficacious as a drug, and when Mother stepped out into the garden and took a deep breath she was already on the way to her cure.

Chapter Four

EXPEDITIONS

We've just been to have Mother's hearing tested and she has had a brilliant time sitting in the chair with her headphones on and informing the audiologist each time she heard a sound, though I'm pretty sure she didn't hear a lot of them. It was a game, one of those 'tests' that she enjoys so much, like scrabble, and if she thought she had won, which she did each time she heard a bleep, she was delighted. The audiologist was a kind man and the little bit of praise he handed out was sufficient to make the whole experience thoroughly enjoyable. Not such good news with her hearing however as there has been significant deterioration.

It is fairly recently that Mother decided she was getting deaf. The problem was, she said, that nobody sounded their consonants properly these days. The nation's speech was getting slovenly and, in particular, people on television were setting an atrocious example. I suppose it was when their vowels disappeared too that she began to think perhaps some of the fault could possibly lie within her own ears.

The National Health Service was scoffed at because, according to village reporting, the waiting lists were too long and anyway the hearing aids were so large and cumbersome that everybody could tell that you were deaf. Being deaf was bad enough, people knowing you were deaf was not acceptable. So a private firm had been selected some years ago and praised for their kind attitude and home service. Kindness sold Mother anything and avoiding the effort of any kind of public transport clinched the deal. A thousand pounds were parted with and everybody started to sound their consonants again.

Hearing aids remind me of Bournemouth in whose theatre my matinee performance in 'French Without Tears' was completely drowned out by the whistling and chirruping of the hearing aids picked up by the tannoy system. Now I heard I the sound once more, this time coming from Mother, and the criticisms of people's appalling articulation habits returned along with my memories. Rather than take action, Mother adopted new behaviours to cope. People have been accused of 'talking across' her at table conversation, of talking so fast she can't understand them. Men are particularly to blame, as are Americans. After some reluctance she accepted the subtitles on television and was satisfied to read these and enjoy criticizing the spelling.

But gradually she has begun to slip into another, far away world when conversation is buzzing around her. A brief concentrated struggle to hear, leaning into the sound with a frown of concentration, willing it to come to her and to make sense, is followed by a relaxation of that tension, a slide back into her chair, and her eyes switching off as her thoughts are going way back and back into some obscure corner of her mind. She becomes vacant, somewhere else far away, in a private world.

Sometimes a word, an expression, perhaps even the shape of someone's lips seeps into her private world, for she will enter the conversation suddenly and make a comment that occasionally is relevant but more often way off beam. Often she will introduce a recently aired subject that has already be chewed over and spat out by the rest of the company. She never seems to notice the puzzled silence that follows as the rest of the speakers try to work out what has just happened and form an appropriate response. What do you do? Is the truth too hurtful? Most people make do with a grunt. Nobody has yet told her to get her hearing tested.

It is easy to see why so much comedy can be created by a deaf character. The wrong word heard resulting in a completely random response, a meaning altered, a comment made out of context turning the conversation bizarre. It's funny. No doubt about it. It's funny on TV, but the desire to laugh at the instigator of the comedy who is sitting in front of you looking frail and confused is so coloured by pathos that the laughter is smothered by guilt and pity.

Since I have been here the private hearing aids have become more or less useless and the correspondence from the firm supplying them more insistent. Not listening at all has become a habit that has isolated Mother further from social interaction and the habit is returned by others around her who have also given up trying to include her. Now that she has become used to my presence she make even less effort to hear and when she is spoken to she immediately turns to me for a repeat of the comment in my familiar and well projected voice.

Under these circumstances a whole culture has developed, especially in the frustrated family, of having conversations that would not have been possible if we thought she could hear them. Talking about her in front of her often becomes the norm and almost an amusing pastime, with the occasional shouted comment in her direction to help her feel she is still in the loop. One gets into the habit of using a kind of précis, refining the spoken words into the most economical sentence or even selecting only the phrase or words that will give the gist of meaning. It has, for her, become a hearing world without nuance, without the adornment of a sentence at all.

In her own communication she now shouts, being unaware of the volume of her own voice, and this makes her sound perpetually angry and the barrage of decibels being thrown at you affects your own relaxation so that irritation is an instinctive reaction. None of the communication is comfortable.

The accumulative effects of deafness, ageing, poor concentration and mobility, result in a narrowing of her whole world. She now can't enjoy normal conversation, she can't watch films or television for long, and people are reluctant to include her as a contributing member of society. And so she has begun to lack a current knowledge of the world, from the great events to the village gossip.

Her sight is not too good either, although this does not appear to have the same impact as deafness, and she complains that taste and smell are diminished too. Loosing sense of taste is a shame as she enjoys food so much, loosing smell worries her. She is afraid that other people will be able to smell her bodily odours and her lifetime habit of frequent bodily washing sometimes now verges on obsession.

I have always thought this element to be lying dormant ready to choose its moment to flourish. I imagine it comes from her generation's beliefs in cleanliness, which was reputed to be next to godliness, for as children we always seemed to be washing for no reason and it was always so uncomfortable.

Thank goodness I no longer have to heave my chilly legs into the sink to wipe them with a flannel laden with Lifebuoy soap and half cold water and then pat them dryish with a slightly damp and cold towel. When old enough to be devious I even devised a ruse to get out of a wash, and also stay out of trouble, by imitating the sounds made on the bathroom floor by the action of washing and swishing just my finger tips in the water. I would never dare tell Mother about this, not even now. However I was luckier with the ritual family bath night which could not be avoided because, being the eldest, I had the water first while it was still warm.

I recently saw a copy of a wartime poster designed to encourage frequent washing. The caption was 'Perspiration is acid – it eats stockings.' No wonder it seeped into the culture of wartime wives and mothers but it has left scar on my own attitude to hygiene. It is of some comfort to me that current thinking is that we have washed our children too thoroughly in the past and have pasteurised all the educational bacteria out of their food. They should have made mud pies and rolled in grass and eaten soil if they wanted to and taught their immune systems to be a little more robust than they are. I'm so glad the only mistreatment I suffered in my childhood was over-washing; it could have been worse.

So with all this deprivation of Mother's senses tumbling towards 'sans everything' it is a little worrying about how to provide what is now known as enrichment as Mother's senses deteriorate. At the moment she is holding her own with a diet of puzzle books, colouring books, TV, historical novels and the incomprehensible pleasure she gets out of the weekly local newspaper which has the least actual news I've ever read. However because she now has my car and my duties as chauffeur she can indulge in a host of stimulating away days with her on-demand expeditions.

***

Mother has always been keen on expeditions and in her younger day put an extraordinary amount of energy into them. In those days it was Mother who did the pushing. She had a large Silver Cross pram which squeaked over the bumps on well built springs and had a middle section in the floor which could be removed, so a child could sit at each end facing each other with two pairs of little legs fitted down in the middle. Mother could often be seen in Summer with a pram full of children, with more children running to keep up at the sides and with a dog attached to the handle by its lead, heading for the river estuary where we lived. It was usually me, being older than the others, who was sent to the bakers for fresh rolls as soon as breakfast was over and the sun was looking reliable. Picnic staples were cucumber and boiled egg rolls trussed up in clean tea towels and put in a canvas beach bag with apples and home made lemonade. Strange nowadays to think of plastic free picnics.

Some days the expedition was to a lonely spot far along the river where we could stomp along the grassy sea wall to frighten away the adders, lie in the long grass one side watching skylarks fly upwards from their nests singing, or, on the other side, slide down the river banks in the silt the tide had left and climb up again looking like black monsters from the haunted lagoon. On autumn days Mother pushed her pram several miles through pastures where we could pick huge mushrooms that grew dotted amongst the cow pats, hoping that one of the brothers would step in one and we girls could then cry out in disgust at them. In the late autumn it was blackberry picking and coming home with purple fingers to make blackberry and apple crumble. Easier pushing for Mother were the lonely, flat roads across the marshes where we could gather glossy conkers and later bake them in the oven to get them really hard ready for conker championships in the school playground.

There was an abundance of nearby beaches she took us to, never sandy, but uncomfortable shingle that we hobbled through to swim while she sat against the stone sea wall on a blanket surrounded by beach bags and towels. There were others with jetties over which we could dangle meat bones to catch crabs and shriek when the naughty boys held the crabs in their fingers and chased us with them. There is one particular beach where I was traumatised at a young age. I was standing on the shingle watching the rough boys splashing in the water when I felt my left leg going hot and put my hand down to feel it. To my horror I saw a little dog, a terrier, who had its leg cocked and was peeing on my leg. I shrieked in disgust and ran to my

Mother, dancing over the shingle and flapping my hands in panic. After that I felt the warm trickle every time we passed that beach. It was wonderful of her to give us children these experiences; not so wonderful I think for her, returning home to abandoned housework and piles of towelling nappies waiting to be washed.

So now I am the one who pushes and I don't think she realises how hard it is to push her wheelchair. I'm completely exhausted and my back is killing me. It's not too bad on the flat, a gradient which is pretty hard to find around here, but uphill, even a very gradual slope, is a terrific strain on your back and your shoulders, and even downhill you are pulling against the gradient to prevent her running away. The ups and downs of kerbs find a totally different set of muscles to torment and steps are completely out of the question. Then there is getting her and the wheelchair out of the car, often from a too small parking space. Anyway I carry on pushing her here, there and everywhere as she requests and attempting to adjust my posture to the new demands made on it.

Sometimes if I stop for any reason she will jerk forward in a childish kind of tantrum, grunting through gritted teeth, as if trying to move the chair herself. I am shocked by the physicality of her reaction. It has an animal quality that is frightening. It infuriates me, I hate her for it. I am doing my best. Why can't she just turn to me and ask if I'm all right? Am I ready to move on? I appreciate that the loss of control over your own life, the loss of the ability to make your own decisions about when you move along and when you pause must be overwhelmingly frustrating. I know that I will be the same if I ever end up in a similar situation but it doesn't stop the anger rising in me and the instinct to retaliate in a similar vein. These are only sometimes moments though, I don't remember anything like them happening when she was younger, maybe just another of the curses of old age.

The reason for my aching back today is that we have been to The Scottish Wool Shop. She has been saying for a while that she needs to go shopping. I use the word 'needs' because it is definitely a need in her. It has nothing to do with a need for items found in shops, it is far more to do with satisfying an emotional need, a hunger for the experience. A relative once told her she was a 'shopaholic' and she was shocked and devastated by it and told the story on numerous

41

occasions afterwards, probably hoping for affirmation that she was not a shopaholic. She retained the propaganda of World War Two, 'Make do and mend says Mrs. Sew and Sew!' and still the idea of buying things she didn't actually need was abhorrent to her. But I understand; a little guilt spread thinly on the conscience makes an activity or indulgence more pleasurable.

Mother was a skilled amateur seamstress and made almost everything we wore as children. Even as a highly critical teenager I approved and even loved the garments she made for me; there were the waspie-belted full skirts of the fifties worn over a stiff petticoat, figure hugging boat necked dresses later for my grammar school dance and a beautiful white and blue organza dress with silver shoulder straps for when an excited teenage me was invited to a May Ball at Cambridge. It was in my period as a would-be ballerina that the only disaster occurred when Mother insisted that a tutu skirt started at the hip when all my friend's tutu skirts started at the waist. I was mortified.

Despite her modest teacher's salary Mother has always looked good in her home-mades and I loved it when she sat at the big table surrounded by the crisp tracing paper of the Simplicity or McCalls dress patterns with the pins in her mouth and the rattling metal foot of her sewing machine with the cotton reel bouncing up and down on its silver spindle. Once when I was little she opened a brown paper parcel on the table and revealed the most exquisite fabric I had ever seen. I know now that it was shot taffeta, shot with dark green and dark blue, but back then I only thought it was like a starling we had found injured one day and nursed back to health. I had seen the bird at close quarters, even touched its amazing feathers than shone out different colours as it shifted on its poor broken leg. In awe I watched the fabric do the same as it moved when she pinned the rustling paper paper pattern to it and then I heard the crunch of the big scissors as she cut through it on the table. The starling fabric lay in weird shaped pieces on the table ready to be transformed.

The next time I saw the starling dress I was in my nightie ready for bed and the baby sitter had arrived. Mother came through the doorway wearing the starling dress with its fitted skirt and a stiff fan bandeau on a strapless bodice and on her feet were black swede high heels. Her hair was curled and her face glowed in powder, rouge, eye shadow and lipstick. I thought she was the most beautiful person I had ever seen.

Forty six years later Mother had given up sewing because her hands weren't capable of fine movements any more and her eyesight was too poor so she gave me her old scrap bag. In it I found, glistening in the middle of all the offcuts, a small piece of the starling fabric. It transported me, and I couldn't help crying for the Mother who had worn the starling dress.

So now she needed to shop for her clothes; a more instant gratification suited to the modern world than the slow skilled process of producing home grown garments. However to fulfil the need to shop she often had to think of something as the focus for the outing, new vests or a warmer blouse, although she had two wardrobes of clothes dating back decades and all in good condition. Today it was tights and possibly a cardigan if she saw one she liked which wasn't too expensive.

Mother is a formidable shopper. In the days when she could walk she would scurry round the dress rails feeling the fabric between her fingers, pulling at the price tags, casting a very critical eye on the design and colour, pulling out a hanger and waving the garment around to examine back and front and occasionally walking to the door with it to compare the colour under both electric and day light. This critical faculty was perhaps the most frightening of all as she would proclaim her judgements in a well projected and expressive voice. The embarrassment this has sometimes caused goes completely unnoticed by her.

On one shopping expedition my daughter had gone to the changing room to try on a garment and Mother, seeing a figure approaching, cried out in disgust 'Good God! Don't get that, it looks dreadful on you!' I immediately apologised to the poor woman who had inadvertently become the subject of Mother's appraisal but Mother just carried on as if nothing had happened. Similar incidents have happened before as Mother has commented on the appearance of a passer by with a 'Good God, look at that!' or 'What is that woman wearing?' in a ringing voice. I understand from the audiologist that a deaf person is unaware of the volume of their own voice which is some comfort to my embarrassment but not helpful to the recipient of Mother's judgements.

Shopping is so much harder with the wheelchair. It's difficult to manoeuvre through the dress racks and she can't see the clothes easily because they are too high up. This means pulling out things she wants to examine further, usually getting the one she didn't mean and getting told off because you didn't know it was the wrong one or being sent back to retrieve an earlier choice that she dismissed but has now changed her mind about. It is very frustrating for her, and for me.

I have done this particular expedition once before and, for the first time ever I think, she left without buying anything. She blamed the shop for not having anything she liked and for going downhill, which is hard to believe as so many of her clothes come from this very shop and it was full of items similar to what is already in her wardrobe. But I think she had found it so tiring that her energy simply ran out.

Today's expedition was more successful as far as the shopping went and she bought some grey trousers, a mauve cable knit jumper, a grey cardigan with pockets and a bottle of Lovage, her favourite tipple when added to Brandy. However the end was rather spoiled by an intervention by a bee. We were making our way to the door past the fancy biscuits when a bee just fell out of the roof and landed on my head. I felt it without realising what it was and brushed my hair to get rid of it. I felt its sting on my finger and at the same time saw it fly away.

Now the last time I got stung by a bee my arm swelled up from finger tip to shoulder and I had to be given antihistamine and steroids, so I assume I have a mild allergy to bees. I said the usual ouch and told Mother what had happened and a woman standing not two yards away heard me and got a packet from her handbag and offered me an antihistamine tablet. What an extraordinary piece of good fortune!

I ran to the café to ask for a glass of water, knowing that an immediate dose of antihistamine might halt the over-reaction of my immune system in its tracks. As it turned out the man behind the counter was the health and safety officer for the store and he insisted on calling 999. I couldn't stop him. I think perhaps he had done all his training and was busting to put it into practice. So now I had the embarrassment of being sat down to wait for the emergency services, with nothing but a mildly swollen finger, in full view of the shoppers who seemed eager for a drama which I really couldn't provide for them. At least they could take home the story of the ambulance car screeching to a halt outside with the blue lights flashing and the siren screaming and they could probably exaggerate the rest to make the story worth telling.

***

My least favourite expedition as a child was the weekly visit to church. I mentioned earlier that I might tell this story and here it is. It starts with forced attendance at church services. I don't think Mother and Max were particularly willing to embrace the full Christian faith; it was part insurance just in case the Christian beliefs were true, especially the ones about heaven and hell, or else a habit that contributed to their status as righteous and conservative citizens. Max was suspicious of our local Vicar and I gathered from overheard adult conversation that he was too 'high Church', having left the Roman Catholics for the Church of England because he wished to denounce his celibacy and marry. I did not understand all of this of course and my objection to going to church was simply on the grounds of utter boredom. We were trussed up in our best every Sunday, walked a mile or so to the ancient Church and squashed into a pew, usually at the back of the cold echoing building. One of my brothers managed to sit furthest away from Mother and Max and was able find relief by reading The Beano without them seeing, but the rest of us had to go through all the standing, sitting and kneeling and droning of the vicar until it was time for release into the sunshine.

As I was the oldest by quite a few years the subject of Catechism came up for me first and I was enrolled in the appropriate class. However, our chaotic family life was such that Mother hardly ever found time to get me to the church on Sunday afternoon for the classes, which could hardly have been a priority for her amongst the weekend washing and four or five other children to take care of, and eventually I got too far behind the other children to take my first communion with them. The Vicar offered to give me individual coaching.

45

Yes, that does sound like a musical hall joke and the ulterior motive that gives the joke its humour was in fact what the Vicar had in mind. At first the solo class was held in the Vicarage, where his timid little wife could be heard bustling about the adjoining rooms He would sit on a large wooden arm chair beside the fire with his Bible on his lap and ask me to stand on his right. After a few minutes he would lay his left hand on his Bible and put his arm round my waist and the arm would gradually drop down until it touched my bare knee. Slowly the hand would rise again from my knee, under my skirt and stroke my thigh up and down.

All the time he would talk about Jesus and the Virgin Mary. All the time my heart would race and my mind become fuzzy. I didn't understand what was happening. Max never really touched me and Mother's touch was loving and gentle and made me feel good. This touch did not. It frightened me, it made me want to shiver, I couldn't hear or see properly. I stood rigid, unable to move.

I tried to get out of my Catechism classes but Mother said I had to go, it was important, and she never asked why I disliked going. In every other learning situation I was always eager, this was the only thing I ever rebelled against, but the alarm bells fell on deaf ears. I believe that the idea that I was being abused would never have occurred to Mother and to disobey her or even question her judgement would not have occurred to me at that age, so I dragged myself along with a disturbing underlying sense of fear.

Later some excuse was made by the Vicar which meant my class was moved from the Vicarage to the Vestry in the empty church. Here, in the dark, lonely room that smelt of incense and musty damp, I was required to sit on his lap for my Catechism with his hand exploring my body inside my skirt. He talked of the Blessed Virgin while I shook with fear of something quite unknown to me.

I knew nothing of sex, I didn't even know what my vagina was for, since anything between our legs was collectively referred to as 'your underneath'. One day during one of these frightening sessions something in me broke, the dam burst. I felt I had lifted out of my own body and all I could do was listen to my own wailing and sobbing echoing round the vestry as if it came from another little girl and not from me. The Vicar got up suddenly and tried to calm me. I was making a lot of noise, hysterical noise, like a wild beast, bouncing off the ancient stones of the vestry walls.

When I had quietened down he led me back into the Church and stood me in front of an life sized, gaudy statue of the Virgin Mary with a scratched blue plaster gown and a chip on one of her plaster fingers. He said it would all be better if we prayed to the Virgin together, so he murmured a prayer and I stood beside him shaking and sobbing and staring at the Virgin's toes through my tears. I can't remember leaving or walking home although I can, to this day, remember feelings and pictures of moments during my ordeal. The droning of Congregational singing makes me nervous, I still have to push down panic when I see a certain type of men's hands. That was the last time I stepped inside a Church apart from unavoidable church weddings and funerals many years later.

To save myself from going to church again I was sick every Sunday morning and somehow the Catechism faded out of Mother's consciousness. Then one day some months afterwards I became hysterical in the kitchen, screaming and falling about, and I have no idea what triggered this release. Mother and Max came running, found me rolling about on the kitchen floor and then pushing myself up against the back door and tried to quiz me about why I was behaving in this extraordinary manner. Max suggested to Mother that perhaps I had 'seen something' and this phrase flashed into my head and came out in my voice. I pointed at the ceiling and cried out that I could see something; the Virgin Mary! Years later I played the part of Mary Warren in Arthur Miller's play The Crucible and did exactly the same thing as Mary Warren and her friends cried out the witches in Salem in response to suggestion.

I eventually calmed down and was sat in an armchair in the living room with a blanket round me while Mother got out of me scraps of information about what had happened at the Catechism classes. They had some difficulty even believing me at first, but the more detail I managed to get out of the hard lump inside me the easier it was for them to see the truth. They were so terribly shocked, Mother crying, desperately sad at what I had endured and probably feeling guilty that she had not realised something was wrong. Max furious with the Vicar, desperate for some action against him but they had no idea what to do about it. I sat in a cold, exhausted state as I listened to

47

them talking about it. I had no feeling for retribution or punishment, I only wanted to be rid of this horrid pain inside my chest.

In the end they did nothing. I don't blame them. How could they complain to the mighty Church of England and the human being ordained by God to be his man on earth? How could they go to our one local policeman whose only contact with us was to ask us not to play cricket in the street? Who could they go to? There were no mechanisms for complaints in those days, no child-line, no specialist police officers or social service officers. So they did what most parents might have done in those days; they brushed it under the carpet and it was never mentioned again. I can't believe that my Mother never thought of it after that day, that she never retraced her steps and thought at what moment should she have intervened, what signs might she have noticed that something was wrong. After all I was never sick from Monday to Saturday, only on a Sunday.

I felt guilty about what had happened to me for many years, later I was able to understand that my guilt was not appropriate. The next stage was when I was able to view the incidents objectively and deconstruct the teachings of the Church which I had taken as the truth because my adults had told me that they were. As an inquisitive sixth former with a burgeoning interest in debating ethics I became a convinced atheist and felt a lot better. It seemed to be my healing was complete.

Perhaps, in those days, obedience was given more reverence than it is now; the virtue of obedience to adults was certainly ingrained in me and it was a major contributor to becoming the 'good girl' I aspired to be. But the good values and ethics, that children should indeed be taught, do not stand up when the adults abuse them.

I have experienced mere 'inappropriate touching', as it is now called, that's all. I was lucky it did not go further and it has not ruined my life. But we know that thousands of children have been abused in a far more damaging way by the clergy and The Church has protected its corrupt ministers with an immorality that beggars belief.

***

I'm tucking into a raspberry Pavlova, my absolute favourite number one choice for a desert. We are in a posh pub by the river and Mother sits next to me. Surrounding us are her friends from the Over Fifties Club; all over fifty is the criteria for membership but it might as well be all over seventy. The three course meal is the climax of the Over Fifties Club annual outing.

We have ploughed up and down the river all afternoon in a gaily painted tour boat with beautiful vistas of woodland creeks, pretty villages and sail boats. Not that the members of the Over Fifties Club have seen much of these wonders as their attention has been ever incarcerated in the varnished wooden interior of the boat, riveted there by the fresh influx of village gossip. Somehow the usual menu of births, deaths and marriages and inappropriate decisions by the Parish Council has been made more pungent by movement across water.

Mother found it difficult to negotiate the wet slip way and then to mount the two wobbling metal steps up to the deck of the boat and clung to me and to the handsome deck hand, digging her nails into my arm and probably into his too. The deck hand, with a disarming smile, said to her 'You're all right. Don't panic my lover.' to which she replied, drawing herself up to as much height as she could manage whilst half way between step and deck, and using her special posh voice 'I don't panic young man. I have never panicked.' This is entirely untrue, she is a prime panicker, everybody knows that, but when her dignity, never mind her safety, is at stake I can't really blame her.

I have been driving her to the Over Fifties Club every Monday afternoon for two o'clock and then collecting her at four. I line up with several other cars waiting for the emergence of the group of grey haired, smiling, Scottish Wool Shop clad ladies with their sticks. It's a wonder we get the right ones into our cars as they all look the same at a distance. They are tired and happy from their game of scrabble, a game at which Mother excels due to her years as an English teacher with a particular gift for spelling. Mother is the scrabble queen and rightly proud of it. Her sister, my auntie Bea, once told me that she likes to write letters to her distant sisters and friends but her letters to my Mother are returned with the spellings corrected. I started to apologise on behalf of my Mother's arrogance when I heard this, but Auntie Bea insisted that it had improved her spelling no end, and she was extremely grateful.

The Over Fifties Club is one of many amenities that are organised usually by volunteers or simply self help groups and this is an admirable feature of village life and one that I never met when I lived in the city. Mother and Max were active for a long time in the twinning with a French village, voluntary work which suited them both as Mother taught French at the school and organised exchanges for the children and Max was a fluent French speaker as well as a fluent drinker of French wine.

Mother has also belonged to a self help art class which flourished without a teacher and simply ran with an apparently democratic critique of each other's efforts, hard to believe I know, as any group in the village is a hot bed for competition as well as gossip. There is also a writing group run on the same lines, although I understand there is more eating of biscuits than there is writing. An arts and crafts group manages to put on a show of their products every month so the village is alive with hand crocheted bonnets and felted bags. I have noticed that there are rather a lot of retired teachers in and around the village and they seem to have fingers in a large number of pies; perhaps a village is an easier and more pleasurable community to organise than a school these days.

These activities are great for retired people although the commitment to them and energy required are as nothing compared to Mother's leisure activities in the past. After she was widowed she was left with me and her teaching job in the small town that was part of the dream which had been extinguished by the war. I suppose there came a time when she realised our life had to go on without my father and she pulled together some colleagues and started an amateur review company that they called The Beachcombers.

Gradually other people joined, probably glad of some light hearted banter and a chance to kick off the misery and austerity of the long war and engage in something creative and productive. They wrote satirical sketches and songs, often with a local theme, made costumes out of crepe paper as there were still shortages of fabric from wartime, constructed scenery and learnt to dance and sing.

The Beachcombers pulled in anybody who had a usable talent, even, for one show, the milkman's horse, who delighted everyone

50

and left a treasured memory for me when it pooped on stage in a musical performance of 'The Circus is in Town'. The milkman's horse's poo was already a celebrity in the town as gathering it from the street to add to the compost was worth threepence to the first child to spot it and collect. The horse was already an experienced entertainer as it was prone to bolt and once turned the corner of our road at speed, throwing crates of bottled milk in all directions, a talking point for some days. However it did not have the notoriety of the Coalman's horse, or, more specifically, the Coalman himself. One Tuesday afternoon it became bored waiting for its owner to emerge from Mrs. Slater's at number twenty eight and began to saunter off when the naked Coalman threw open the bedroom window and shouted to it to stop.

The Beachcombers, led by my intrepid Mother, were indomitable; they built stage buses and moving roundabouts, they larked about under plywood palms in grass skirts, they defied every sensible limitation and just enjoyed themselves, and so did their audiences. They were a hit. Children of the performers and backstage crew were not excluded; partly because they added a certain cuteness factor for the audience and partly, and this is just my own guess, because their inclusion limited the need for baby sitters. I didn't mind the dressing up, the dancing, the adult company, the applause. Why should I? I got the bug, I still have it. And I was proud and special because my Mother was the boss.

It was in the Beachcombers company that Mother met Max, who by all accounts was a slick performer and remarkably handsome, but as Mother's interest gradually transferred to more serious acting in local amateur dramatic companies, his fell away and although they married I don't think they appeared again together after Beachcombers eventually expired. It was also in Beachcombers that I first felt the thrill of being on a stage. I was dressed in white satin with a flouncing skirt overlaid with pink satin petals and a pink satin petal hat as I danced into a magical world to the tune of The Sugar Plum Fairy.

Mother was particular about our reading material. Enid Blyton's adventurous five were rejected on the grounds of faulty grammar in favour of Arthur Ransome's sensible and well spoken four. The Beano and Dandy were banned in favour of The Eagle and The Girl and it was within The Girl that I found my inspiration in Belle of the Ballet. Standing in front of my wardrobe mirror and scraping back my hair and adopting her pouting lips I felt I could almost be mistaken for her. I longed to join the world of The Ballet.

Mother was keen for me to go far in my dancing career. Originally I was given the choice to properly learn either dancing or piano, but I had heard the ghastly noises of piano lessons through the wall between us and the piano teacher next door, and so I chose dancing.

I was sent to the same dancing school as Mother's friend's daughter so that I could be looked after on the fifteen minute bus ride and together we went every Saturday to study with Madame Jones, a very strict ballet mistress of the old school. A leg not fully turned out or a toe not completely pointed would result in a sharp tap with her cane on our calf muscle. When the money got tight Mother sent me to the local teacher, local always being seen as a quality step down from away and cheaper.

Mrs. Tucker, wife of the fishmonger, took private lessons above the shop with smell of fish wafting up the stairs. She was a large woman with wobbly breasts and bottom and she plonked away at the upright piano shouting out positions of the arms as we did our barre exercises holding onto the back of her dining chairs. Her face was kind but had a slight resemblance to a cod although whether it came from living above the shop or was her natural feature I didn't know. I rather favoured the former because on the wall of her sitting room come studio was a black and white photographic portrait of a beautiful dancer in an arabesque position which was too reminiscent of her as a young, slim woman to be dismissed.

Eventually her business bloomed and she hired the village hall for classes and it was here that my skills at ballet, tap and modern were honed right up until the age of eighteen when I left for drama school. Acting as a career was my second choice. My crying over the music of Swan Lake, my drooling over black and white photographs of Galina Ulanova in my Ballet Annual, my emulation of Belle of the Ballet, came to a crushing end when I was examined for a place at the Royal Ballet School and told my skeleton, especially ankles, were not up to it. Being a supreme optimist I decided to be an actor instead and have never regretted it and have never forgotten the part my Mother played in giving me these opportunities.

***

Sitting as I am now in the midst of the Over Fifties Club veterans and their elaborate puddings it is hard to imagine the joyful antics that are held in their memories. Because I have shared so much of Mother's life I am witness to many of hers, but I wonder who will be guardian of theirs. I desperately want to gather their memories while they are still the treasured fruits of their lives and preserve them before they fall and decay and are lost forever.

I am the last to finish my raspberry Pavlova and I have savoured every wonderful mouthful. I was once singing with my band and as usual the musicians were housed in the same marquee as the caterers. Spread upon the trestle table after the buffet were rows of Raspberry Pavlovas. I cannot imagine why the guest were not hungry for them. The catering manager told me that if the Pavlovas were not eaten they would be thrown away. A travesty! I saw a young woman approaching with a black bin bag. I managed to eat five one after the other before the bin bag devoured them and then I went on to sing the second set. I think it enhanced my reputation.

Now the annual outing of the Over Fifties Club is almost at an end. We are onto the coffee, every mouthful on every plate has been consumed, despite the cries of astonishment at the size of the portions and the protestations that a portion that big could never be finished. But this is the waste not want not generation so at the finale all plates are clean. The bill has been prepaid months ago. It hardly needs arranging as this outing is repeated in its every detail every year. The Over Fifties Club is comfortingly predictable.

Chapter Five

WATERSHED

It has been a dreadful day. Suddenly nothing is as it was, everything has changed. These days rarely come in a lifetime but here is one, well, there was one, because the day is almost over now. I'm absolutely freezing, standing at a bus stop outside the hospital without a coat having no idea when a bus will come to get me home.

Yesterday was bad too. We have had nothing but trouble with the tenants in our house and now we get a call from the estate agent to say they have gone and the ceiling over the stairs has fallen in. I can't get to Manchester and leave Mother, the profit we had hoped for has gone in repairs and now we will have to sell the house at a loss. That was yesterday.

Today started with promise and a phone call. At last we had persuaded Mother to have a timer switch put on the immersion heater and Charlie the electrician just happened to be on the end of the phone and was able to come that very morning to do the work. As Charlie knocked on the door I glanced at the washing machine and saw it had only a few minutes to the end of the wash, so Joe took Charlie upstairs while I made Mother promise not to try to take the clean washing out of the machine, knowing that she had neither the strength nor the balance to do it safely. I needed to be part of the important discussion to decide the point of fixture for the switch, so I joined the two of them upstairs as they were having a quiet giggle about Mother and her use of electrical devices.

In the case of the immersion heater her habit had been to switch it on as she left the bathroom after her early morning wee so that the water would be hot for washing as soon as she had eaten her breakfast and after washing she would switch it off. She had long decided it was not worth the cost of getting the heater's broken thermostat mended when she could govern the operation so easily, but since her memory had deteriorated she regularly forgot to switch it off again. I don't know what happened before we came, but once here we were often alerted by the sound of boiling water in the tank and had to divert yet another catastrophe. So another positive notch on the state of our peaceful minds was about to be carved by replacing Mother's dangerous habits with reliable technology.

As Joe, Charlie and I giggled upstairs at the start of this day, there was a cry from below. It wasn't all that loud but something about it made it stunningly clear that it was urgent, so I hurried downstairs to find Mother lying on the floor clutching a wet duvet cover with her head jammed up against the fridge. There was no blood, merely a quiet whimper of noise, but her left leg was turned out at a most unnatural angle from her body.

We managed to get a cushion under her heard and replace the wet duvet cover with a dry blanket. It was quite obvious that she should not be moved because it looked as if her leg would not move with her body, it hardly seemed to be attached to her. Joe had already dialled 999 and handed the phone to me. The 999 call is so frustrating because you have to go through what seems like an interminable questionnaire about the condition and vital signs, all necessary I know, but all you want to say is 'Get me some help! Quickly!'

Help did arrive quickly in the form of the local first responder who began to assess the situation and he was followed by a paramedic in a car. I saw the car draw up and my immediate response was to say to the driver 'You won't get her in a car!', not remembering that to get to us out here in the sticks an ambulance has several miles to travel each side of a ferry, it's a kind of three tier response; first responder, paramedic in car, and later an ambulance.

Before long the kitchen was full of people. Charlie was saying goodbye before making a wise retreat, Cilla, Mother's cleaner, had just arrived, so there were four medics and Joe, Cilla and me and Mother, who by now was in pain and groaning.

I think they gave her morphine, although the shock, the stress of those minutes has blurred my memory even though it was only this morning, but she didn't quieten down. The paramedic said something but his voice seemed to me to be far away and it was a second before I realised he had said 'She's done her hip.' It wasn't as if he had said something ordinary, something merely informative to the other men crowded round Mother. The tone was loaded and that, along with the expressions on all the men's faces and the atmosphere being so tense and heavy, made me realise this wasn't just another fall but something which possibly had consequences. Everything was heightened, fast moving in slow motion, panicked and yet solemn. Joe and Cilla stood at the kitchen door with the bag they had got together for hospital. They looked white and stunned.

Getting Mother onto a stretcher was achieved really quickly in one expert move but she cried out in pain and groaned horribly. Then they realised that the positioning of the kitchen door and the exterior door were too awkward to get a stretcher through and they had to carry her out into the cold garden in the drizzle and through the garden gate to the ambulance which was parked blocking the road with a car already lined up waiting to pass.

I sat silently in the ambulance while the paramedic was going through his routine methodically and calmly and glancing constantly at the graphs and figures that were flicking and changing on the monitor screens. I heard him say her blood pressure was off the scale. It is twenty six miles to the hospital through narrow lanes, a ferry crossing and traffic hold-ups. It's a long way under these circumstances and the ambulance was bumpy; I thought it would have better suspension. I kept imagining the broken bones in Mother's hip being jolted, jutting into the surrounding flesh and nerves, scraping into each other. I remembered the x-ray I saw from my own broken arm with the ends of the bone laying side by side in stead of joining in a vertical straight line and I remembered the pain of it. I was grateful that Mother seemed drugged, her reaction subdued, and hoped her mind, her senses, were far, far away.

There was a short wait in the corridor and a long wait once she was transferred to a cubicle. Nobody came for ages as I stood by the bed holding her hand. She hadn't spoken since she lay on the kitchen floor, she hadn't asked a question or tried to tell me she was all right which she always did no matter what was wrong with her. She was drifting somewhere else.

There was a calm bustle outside the cubicle, people swishing the blue paper curtains open and closed, referring to computers, writing on pads, consulting with each other. A thin young man in a white coat came in and said the consultant would be here soon. I asked what would happen if her hip was broken and he said he was a junior but he thought treatment would be either to operate or, if she was too weak, to leave it. Leave it? Did he mean simply leave her with her bones broken apart and the flesh torn? Leave her unable to walk? Leave her because she was too old to bother with? Leave her because she was no longer useful? Leave her to die? I didn't know how to ask all these hideous questions, I couldn't form something which encompassed all my fears and so I just said 'Will she be all right?' He simply repeated that the consultant would be here soon.

I was so glad the consultant did come soon so that my ridiculous imagination was given no more time to create scenarios of doom. He was broad shouldered with a shock of black hair and just the kind of phlegmatic I needed to calm my racing pulse. He explained to me that Mother was not in pain and would need an x-ray before any decisions about treatment could be made and he asked the nurse who stood by him to prepare her. The preparation consisted of cutting off her clothes and I watched as two young nurses, one each side of her, deftly slipped their scissors through the bottom of each trouser leg and snipped their way to the waistband in a masterly action. I cringed as they began their work on the lilac lambswool jumper we had bought for her only yesterday. How different our world was then as we delighted in our choice in the Edinburgh Wool shop, little knowing what twenty four hours could bring, never imagining that the lilac lambswool jumper would be wrecked by the following day in this strange ritualistic fashion.

So there she lay, barely conscious I think, with her clothes peeled away to each side of her and before they covered her I saw her legs, one lying in perfect unison with her body and the other, with no outward sign of injury and aligned in parallel with the first, but twisted so that her knee and foot lay at a right angle away from her body.

They wheeled her away and I sat and waited and watched as the strange activity of A & E continued relentlessly. I felt as if I were in a film, that none of this was real, that I had imagined it all and someone would soon tap me on the shoulder and tell me to go home and stop building these stupid scenarios in my mind. But the person who did interrupt my reverie was the consultant who took me to look

57

at the x-ray of Mother's poor deformed hip joint. They would have to replace the ball that fits into the socket and part of her femur with steel. Surgery was urgent, he explained, and there was a risk because of her age and condition. He urged me to go home as Mother would not be properly awake for a long time and since there was nothing I could do to help it would be better to be rested when she woke up.

It was dark when I stepped out of the hospital doors and the rain was lashing in the yellow light of the street lamps. I hadn't thought about a coat, or something to eat when I left home all those hours ago but I did have my purse so I knew that if the worst came to the worst I could get a taxi from somewhere. I saw the row of bus shelters not far away, at least a bus could get me part of the way home, but I've been waiting now for twenty minutes in the cold, wet night.

***

I am trying to work out what had happened, to go over every detail and make some sense of it. If only Mother had listened to me, heeded my warning and left the duvet cover for me to pull out of the washing machine. Why didn't she? What made her stagger up from her chair, walk around towards the machine holding on to the table and then pull at the duvet cover to get it out? Was there sudden exasperation that the finished washing had not been taken out as it should have been? Was there an annoyance that people thought she wasn't capable of doing it? Was there a flicker of anger that I was treating her as a child and 'telling her off'? I imagined that in her irritation she has tugged at the cover because it was caught in the door of the machine and it has suddenly given way and over-balanced her. In that swift and unconceived moment in time an insignificant event has happened which has precipitated a significant and possibly life changing result.

How will our lives change now? Will Mother die? What will Joe and I do if she does? Will we go home to Manchester? We have made no plans, we have been too busy making our lives right with Mother to even think about the next move. Surely they would not have suggested I go home if they thought that Mother was about to die. They must believe that she can survive this surgery but I have

58

heard that a broken hip is often the beginning of a decline, that very few older people live a year or more after such an accident in which case what are the immediate challenges that will face us? When Mother has been in hospital for lesser problems they have said that she wouldn't be discharged unless a care plan was in place and her condition was manageable for us so perhaps she will be in hospital for a while to give us a chance to get ready for her return home.

***

Mother has been moved to the cottage hospital fifteen miles away following her hip surgery. It is a modern building nestled amongst the hills and has spacious walkways and huge picture windows. Inside the ambience is peaceful with no sense of urgency or trauma. But I am very concerned that whilst it is very pleasant there and she has eaten well and is obviously better in health than when she arrived a full two months ago, nothing has really been done to aid recovery. I was told the hospital specialised in convalescence and she would receive physiotherapy to get her walking again. So far she has hardly been out of bed. I am worried that they have given up on her because what I see looks very much like palliative care.

After the operation at the main hospital the atmosphere was tense; she was only there for a few days and I wasn't able to see the surgeon, but the junior doctors and nurses seemed evasive and only gave the stock medical assurance answers to my questions when I wanted detail and some kind of prognosis. The day she was due to leave by ambulance for the cottage hospital the anaesthetist came to see the woman in the next bed and came to exchange a few words with Mother to see how she was. Mother was of course delighted to have the attention of this charming tousled haired young man and I was pleased to see her smiling again. I introduced myself as her daughter and he told me, casually, almost as if I already knew, that he wouldn't want to do that operation again. I felt as if I'd been hit in the chest. What weren't they telling me? I had to know and I tried to probe him for some more information as diplomatically as possible.

He told me they weren't sure she was fit enough to take the surgery but there was a risk of her dying either way and when the situation suddenly became urgent they decided to go ahead. Why did they send me home? Surely I should have stayed if it was that uncertain. Perhaps I should have realised and been more assertive, made my own decision about whether to stay. Through my whirling thoughts I heard him say they almost lost her and had to hurry the operation. He said she should never have a general anaesthetic again, she may not survive it. He didn't mention it at the time but now I know that one of her legs is considerably shorter than the other; helping her out of bed some time ago I thought I had imagined it, or that her hips were at an angle but then I saw that her knees didn't line up together.

I realise that having legs of different lengths is going to cause all sorts of strains throughout her body if she is able to walk again. She needs to be taught to compensate or to favour different parts of her mechanism or weight, I don't know what, but I do know she needs to keep moving and she needs help. When I broke my arm I didn't get a great deal of help from the NHS to recover but I was teaching at drama school at the time and we had a fearsome physiotherapist to run an injury clinic for the student actors, whose classes in Circus Skills often called for post-class physiotherapy skills. I went to him because my wrist had more or less seized up and I learned that if you don't keep moving injured parts, even though it means squealing through the pain barrier, you are likely to lose use of it – use it or lose it!

I spoke to the person in charge of the ward about physiotherapy and was told they were arranging it but when I asked Mother some days later she said someone had been and examined her walking but had not come back. I know she has been taken out of bed onto a turntable and transferred to a commode and has tried a few steps with a walking frame, but that doesn't sound like physiotherapy. I don't know who to believe.

At home we are in limbo. There have been so many 'will she won't she?' moments which make it very hard to live in the present which is known to be the best way to stay sane. She didn't die but she hasn't recovered, she might be mobile but she isn't so far, she might be able to come home but she might have to be found residential care. I spend a large proportion of my time travelling to and from the hospital leaving Joe to muddle through on his own. Nothing gets done properly. We live in a mental state of heightened drama with dreams full of ambulances, white coats, drawn faces, knowing that Mother is struggling weakly through it with her wartime bomb shelter stoicism, trying to not be a bother to anyone. I wish she could come home, I feel we are so out of control. I'm sure she would get better more quickly if we could downsize from this great rushing, bustling, secretive, overwhelming machine that is the hospital service, downsize to a more homely, patient focussed environment, one that had familiar faces and straight talk.

I have thought a lot lately about how healthy Mother has been all her life. It isn't that she has had an easy life because she hasn't; she has endured troubling times for the country and personally, her marital relationships have been blighted with bad luck, she has birthed and bred six children and supported them faithfully through their own problems and, apart from a hysterectomy that she never mentions, the only health problem I can recall was recurring 'sick headaches' as she used to call them. They always seemed to come on Saturday so were probably caused by stress as the working week finished. Now she is taking her recovery from this serious accident in her stride, grateful for every crumb of support given.

I know I keep sighting the war as shaping attitudes but it seems to often be an appropriate explanation. Apart from my father's death, all Mother's war stories are fun, she even laughs when telling me she used to stuff me under a cushion when the bombers came overhead; a cushion versus the the might of the German Luftwaffe! More often she tells of dancing to the great dance bands at the Hippodrome, of romances with handsome boys, camaraderie between girlfriends and whispered conversations between her sisters in bed at night to establish who had let who do what to them.

Mother and her sisters always practised the philosophy of 'looking on the bright side' so it could have been a family gene that is responsible for Mother's selective memories and, since I am often accused of inflated optimism by my children, the gene has now manifested itself in me. Mother and her sisters often enjoy a repeat of this particular war story. They were in the air raid shelter at the bottom of my Granddad's garden in Lewisham and they heard the all clear sounding. It had been a lovely sunny day so they were surprised to find on emerging that it was raining, the rain dripping off their plum tree, so they had to run through the garden to the shelter of the

61

house. However it wasn't raining at the front of the house. Then they realised that a German bomb had exploded in next door's fish pond and the water from it was dropping from the trees. Well, wasn't that funny?! Nobody in the telling of the tale ever remarks that had the bomb dropped two yards west they would have lost their house or two yards north and their neighbours would have been killed in their basement.

I think of Mother's sisters, those two lovely aunties, always joking, giggling, making up funny rhymes and pulling silly faces to amuse me when I was a child. They shared a bedroom and it was a place of wonder for me. There were high heels in the wardrobe, fancy bras in the drawers, stockings and suspenders and on the dressing table was a glass bottle with a woven cable leading to a rubber ball and when you pressed it sweet perfume sprayed out of the nozzle at the top. The top of the table was glass and underneath were crocheted mats and, on top, golden tubes of lipstick and jars of white cream and little pads of red rouge and blue eye shadow and large tubs of pink powder and fluffy powder puffs. No wonder they always looked so beautiful. Once they put two little patches of rouge on my face and I stared in the mirror at my pink cheeks with a little tickle of excitement in my tummy at my potential transformation into a beauty. Now these lively young ladies are old, not as old as Mother, but subdued by age, but sometimes, just for a short while, you see them as you remember them in their youth.

**

It is some time ago now that Mother was discharged from hospital to home. Mother still could not walk but could manage to transfer from bed to wheelchair and from wheel chair to commode with the help of one person and a walking frame; that seemed sufficient for me to manage her at home but the arrangement of rooms and furniture at home would need rethinking. After inspection the two nurses, whose job was to create the care plan, decided it would be impossible for her to use her upstairs bedroom because although she already had a stair lift there were two additional steps which she would not be able to manage. The sitting room downstairs should be arranged for her to occupy day and night.

This took a little time during which Mother stayed impatiently in the cottage hospital while we organised disposal of sofas and chairs, all of which were too big to manoeuvre through the tiny spaces round the door. We had to call a builder to take the window out and all the furniture went through the gap into the narrow road, dodging the traffic. Her bed was dismantled and re-mantled downstairs, a commode arrived in a social services truck and, for modesty, I bought a bamboo screen to aid privacy from the window to the street and door to the kitchen. Mother came home.

We didn't have much interference from anybody. Madge visited a few times, each time bringing a little potted plant for Mother, and the two of them talked gardening for a while. As I listened from the kitchen I wondered if Mother would ever get out in the garden again, but the subject didn't enter their conversation. The district nurse came and everything was judged to be progressing except the amount of pain she was having. The GP prescribed, in addition to paracetamol, some transdermal patches which would release morphine continuously and although she showed some relief from the pain it wasn't complete.

The hospital had made appointments at the physiotherapy clinic but I was expected to provide transport. Getting her first into the wheelchair and then through the door of the house was difficult enough but getting her out of the wheelchair and into the car was a nightmare! At first I could not work out how to do it. Once lifted from the wheelchair she couldn't stand on her bad leg so I had to hold her up and then lower her on to the seat and then hold her bad leg while I twisted her and got the good leg into the foot well. Then there was no other way than to bend her bad leg at the knee, which made her yell, and tuck her foot down next to the other one. By this time she was feeling sick. Having got to the hospital and parked as near the entrance as possible I had no idea how to get her out and went to the reception to get help. Apparently there was no person who's job description covered getting patients out of their cars, apparently you can't do it without training, so I wondered how they thought I was managing, I hadn't even acted this one before! Eventually they found a willing person and evacuation from my Ford Fiesta was achieved. I was extremely concerned that this

63

process was likely to injure either Mother or myself and thus require even more physiotherapy.

The physiotherapist was a courteous and patient woman but unfortunately she had little effect on Mother who forgot the exercises as soon as she got home, which isn't surprising since the whole effort of getting there and back was torturous and aggravated Mother's injury rather than sped recovery. I spoke to the GP and an arrangement was made for sessions at home; these lasted only a few weeks. Mother was charmingly co-operative while the therapist was there but it was a case of once out of sight out of mind and ended with me nagging Mother to do her exercises. Sometimes, just as I walked into the room, she would start flapping her feet around in a random way, pretending that she had been doing her exercises for ages, although I did not recognise these flappings as something the physiotherapist recommended! I did not know my Mother could be so devious! When I tried to help her with them she became childish and it all ended in an argument. I mentioned all this to the GP who shook his head and confirmed that this was a quite usual reaction and told me not to worry.

Despite an absence of physiotherapy Mother is now ready to venture upstairs to her bedroom at night by means of the chair lift on the stairs and a walking frame at each end. A lorry arrived from social services with various pieces of equipment; a second commode for upstairs, a hospital bed, a table that swung across the bed and an air mattress and a lovely man called Bob who put up copious grab rails. The sitting room window was taken out again because the sitting room had to return to its proper function and we had to bring in a new sofa, the old one having been given away to make room for Mother's old bed which was now about to follow the old sofa through the window to pastures new.

The commode was to stay, as was the screen I had bought to make a modesty barrier, which Mother had never used as she was quite oblivious to passers by right next to the window and people in the kitchen separated by only a curtain. The curtain did succeed in hiding the sight of Mother on the commode but was not so effective with the sounds. The commode was my worst job, particularly having to empty it frequently in case the bouquet in the sitting room became undesirable, and also because Mother's aim was not too accurate and it was situated over a thick fitted carpet. A toilet roll had been replaced by separate tissues which could be used with one hand and, owing to Mother's now inaccurate throw, they were often scattered far and wide. On one occasion she forgot to take the lid off the pot when going for a wee and wondered why there was a water feature beneath her.

I usually help her onto the commode and then withdraw to allow her some privacy and this has allowed her another delightful trick. Mother's confection of choice is chocolate éclairs and she always has some handy despite her protestations that she hardly ever eats any sweets and her diet is especially healthy. However, one day when I waited in the kitchen for her to finish I could hear the distinctive rustle of sweet papers and I peeped through the curtain to see her sitting happily on the commode stuffing chocolate éclairs into her mouth and hiding the papers in her pocket. Of course I would find them later, how did this not occur to her? I never took her up on this; it seemed a shame to spoil her pleasure in indulgence, and, after all, what harm could a few sweets do at her age? I know from experience how much tastier a treat is when laced with guilt. My weakness is cream and I often keep a special tub of Cornish Clotted cream in the fridge which I call my 'Stealing Cream' and which I take out surreptitiously and wipe my finger round the tub then straight into my mouth. It tastes so delicious that way and I explain to myself that the joy of duplicity without harm or guilt is therapeutic for me.

So now Mother is upstairs at night and downstairs during the day and we have settled to some kind of routine, but it seems like quite hard work; she needs help with any kind of movement and dressing is very awkward. I feel that I don't know what I'm doing as quite often she yells out as I try to manoeuvre her. The doctor has been a few times because they are still trying to deal with the amount of pain she is experiencing. He suggested I should get some help with her, perhaps to do the showering which is now positively dangerous as she tries to step over the one foot high entrance to her 'walk in shower' hanging onto me and the rail that Bob put in. The construction of her 'modern' bathroom is yet another example of an elderly person being exploited as the installer, instead of cutting the shower base into the floor so it was in fact a 'walk-in' shower, level with the floor, took an easier option and plonked the base on top of the floorboards, giving Mother a foot high step up and over into the shower.

The shower is another of the things I don't like doing. Mother doesn't appear to mind baring all, but I fine it distressing and would rather not see it. I am still shocked by her poor old body, she is so thin and wasted and it increases my awareness of her vulnerability. It still feels disrespectful to touch her naked body. The shower is probably the one time that Mother pulls out all her physical resources and she attacks the task with a vigour that used to be reserved for gardening.

Gripping Bob's rail with one hand she takes the pre-soaped flannel from me and scrubs in a feverish haste while I re-soap when needed and do the bits she can't reach. She prefers a big towel for drying, old habits die hard, but as you can imagine it is not easy to handle a big towel with one hand when you can hardly stand up, so it is more of a token dry to be finished off by myself with a fresh towel because she has dropped her towel on the wet shower base too many times. The whole shower experience is terrifying and every time when we have completed it without an accident happening I heave a sigh of relief. Mother always needs to sleep afterwards.

The district nurse said it would be great for me to get carers who could do the shower while I was downstairs getting the breakfast or even just sitting having a well earned cup of coffee. So I arranged for carers to do the shower three times a week, I say carers in the plural because they insisted that the job was impossible for one person. I suppose they had to think of liability and litigation if one lone carer let Mother fall, a problem I, apparently, don't have.

The young women were really kind people but firstly they didn't come until eleven o'clock, sometimes later, by which time Mother was steaming because she was still in bed and missing out on all sorts like watching the birds breakfasting. Obviously it was easier to get her in and out of the shower with two people but I felt odd sitting downstairs while they did it. I felt too tense to get on with anything else and was completely unproductive as I listened to their squeaky carer's voices, always two notes higher than normal speech, as they encouraged Mother along with their specialist vocabulary; 'there we go' 'well done' 'that was nice wasn't it?' 'you feel better now' and so on. Mother seemed quite happy with this mode of communication which is both encouraging and patronising but I can't imagine myself being quite so patient when my turn comes. It was also very expensive and what with all this irritation I decided to stop it and carry on myself.

I thought that now that we had established some kind of routine it might be time to take another step forward, perhaps to start going out in the car again or to the Over Fifties Club. But Mother has decided that she doesn't want to go to the Over Fifties Club any more. I have tried to persuade her that I could drive her to the door, she could get upstairs as there is a chair lift there and she could sit in her wheelchair at the scrabble table and I'm sure her friends would welcome her with open arms. But no, she doesn't want to go and that's it. I do worry that it will be a significant step to take since it may cut off almost all her social interaction and I don't believe her friends, all of whom are elderly, will make the effort to visit her at home which is the other end of the village. I wonder if she feels she is not the same person as she was when last there, that she feels disabled, and being disabled is not a part of her personality that she understands.

Chapter Six

STRANGE HAPPENINGS

I think I need something for myself, a temporary escape, a bolt hole. Yes that's it! A rabbit hole to fall down, like Alice did, to find a fantasy world where nothing is the same as the world above ground. I know from past experience as an actor that I am very happy living in a fantasy world, after all I have spent most of my life pretending to be other people and I find them far more interesting than myself. I am happiest being a conduit for the expression of others. But how to achieve it? Most theatre is a collaborative art form involving writers, directors, actors and audiences, although even I have ventured into the one woman show as a storyteller.

One of my storytelling adventures was in Infant schools; after many years of Theatre in Education I felt that the infants were always left out and they had such potential as audience since up to the age of seven they are able to suspend belief and allow themselves extraordinary journeys of the imagination. It became one of my most enjoyable gigs. I carried the whole show, props and costumes, in a suitcase in my old Ford Fiesta and got changed at the school. The fact that it was odd came as a sudden revelation as I peeped out from amongst bean bags and hula hoops in the dimly lit gym cupboard to watch the excited audience filing in to sit cross legged in rows.

My inner voice suddenly cried out 'What am I doing!?' as I realised I had spent thirty years creating original and applauded performances on stage and film in the company of many fine practitioners and here I stood waiting, alone, for my entrance in a gym cupboard that smelt of musty infant sweat. No mirror framed with bright light bulbs, no good luck cards wedged into the frame, no smell of Leichner greasepaint. I am an actor who had a proper dressing room in my early twenties. I have shared a luxurious

Winnebago trailer with a Dame. What am I doing in a Gym cupboard?

Don't get me wrong, I love working with children and in community theatre, but this dressing room experience will never have been even imagined by almost all of my ex-colleagues. Perhaps I should mention that this dressing room has only ever been beaten for top place on the awards list by one other, which was in a rural community show when the well meaning Village Hall Committee offered the acting company a unique dressing room experience in an outhouse full of smelly rabbits in hutches.

In any case, thinking about acting now is out of the question. There simply aren't the opportunities to work as an actor in this location and besides I feel the need to be more anonymous than I was as an actor; I am a little tired of putting myself up for public scrutiny. A painter doesn't need to reveal herself and her emotional knowledge in front of a live audience. I need something which I can stop or interrupt if needed at home and I am wondering about painting. I used to paint, I even scraped through A level art, but it was a long time ago and the only paint brush I've picked up since is a decorator's brush. But if I went to class I would be the student, I would be learning, I wouldn't be expected to be at the top of my game. I wouldn't need to show anyone what I'd done. Painting could be a solitary occupation and could be done at home while Mother slept if needed. I remember now that Mother started painting when she was seventy; it must be in the genes. I will enrol on this new venture as soon as possible.

***

I'm getting really worried about the amount of pain Mother is having. The only time she is anything like comfortable is when she is lying perfectly still and even then she feels it. She has spent so much time lying on her back that she has developed pressure sores and we now have visits from the district nurse to treat them. She can't lie on either side because of pain and any movement causes her to cry out. Now my Mother is not one to complain, she simply puts up with problems, so I know that if she does complain there is something really wrong. The pain has meant that the GP has had to

69

incrementally increase the amount of pain killing drugs she has but has now finally agreed that something may be amiss and arranged for an x-ray at the cottage hospital.

It was a nightmare getting her onto the x-ray table. The radiographer was so kind and allowed me to stay in the room to comfort Mother and informed me of every step he was taking. Later he let me see the x-ray. I saw the metal ball the surgeons had put in her, brilliant white in the creamy grey picture, and then a white tapering spike running through the middle of her femur. All of that was expected to be there; what wasn't expected was a white bone mass like a flowery choral blooming from her injured hip joint.

One theory suggested was that her inactivity, the absence of physiotherapy or movement had aggravated this phenomena. There was a suggestion that a possible solution was surgery to remove the growth, but after the report from the anaesthetist it was obvious that she wouldn't cope with another general anaesthetic. What actually happened was the regime of strong painkilling drugs was to be continued. So we struggle on with Mother getting noticeably more drugged up; she sleeps longer and more deeply, and in the parts of the day where she used to be awake she drops off frequently and if I accidentally wake her she is startled and pretends she wasn't asleep at all as if she feels guilty for wasting the day. I feel sad that the times she is alert and living are getting shorter and this marks yet another decline in her quality of life.

***

The art class did turn out to be the right choice for my leisure activity for exactly the reasons that I anticipated. The interruption I expected actually came during the class as I was most of the way through a self portrait. My phone rang and it was Joe asking me to come home. The expression in the self portrait was quite pleasing, rather calm for me, and thoughtful, and was nothing like the expression of alarm on my face when Joe told me what was happening at home. Mother had become very agitated because she heard a woman singing loudly in the street outside the house. She had sent Joe out twice to ask the offender to move on but he saw nobody there. She had then struggled from room to room on her walking frame because she could hear strangers talking. Joe had tried to stop her getting out into the road and she had been abusive. By the time I got home she was seeing little boys walking through the sitting room wall.

I don't know why I didn't call a doctor. Maybe it was because the bizarre behaviour I observed didn't have the characteristics of an emergency; Mother seemed quite happy once she had got used to it, at times she even enjoyed it, the only annoyance for her seemed to be that we couldn't see and hear what she could. It almost felt as if she thought we were playing some sort of joke on her by saying we couldn't see people walking through walls or staring through the front window. I was once told that when elderly people are confused it is better to go along with their odd notions rather than try to correct their perception, so we just monitored her condition and blamed the heavy dose of painkillers she was taking.

I hardly slept that night as I could hear her talking and several times I crept downstairs from our attic bedroom to listen at her door. She was talking to imaginary friends. This has never hurt children so, although anxious at her odd behaviour, I returned to bed. In the morning I called for second opinions from Kit and Roz who drove over to us to observe. It was getting hilarious; Mother was having a great time, thoroughly enjoying the explosion of entertainment unfolding before her eyes and ears. There were Brownies destroying the wardrobe, the bedroom walls were painting themselves in kaleidoscopic colours, there were cows in the attic and Brian next door was singing at the top of his voice. This last one didn't please Mother so much as he was singing the wrong words and we were asked to knock on his door to complain.

Although we could find no explanations it was good for me that I had other people to take a turn in the crazy world of Mother's bedroom while I had a rest and eventually we made a joint decision to wait until morning unless her condition changed. That night she didn't sleep at all. I know it is easy to say oh I didn't sleep a wink last night but this was real, no sleep at all. Instead she was full of energy, wild with excitement, seeing herds of singing lizards stampeding down the hill, seeing walls fade in and out to allow the hoards of visitors into the room, hearing choirs that drifted across the ceiling. I had to bring a chair into the room to sit with her and she related the scenes to me as they trundled by. Twice she tried to get out of bed to go to work despite the fact that she still could not stand alone. It seemed that all pain and disability had vanished with the fantasies.

In the morning I called the doctor and he booked a place for her in the nursing home and called an ambulance which took an age to come. We managed to get her downstairs and I really don't think she was in the real world at all by then. When the medics arrived the driver went into the room where she was sitting and leant towards her with a kindly, gentle demeanour. She looked him fiercely in the eye and said 'It's about time you've come!' He hardly began his apology when she continued 'I want you to take your children out of here at once. They've been very naughty. They're in my chimney trying to get a piano down it.'

They had to strap her in the chair securely because she fought tooth and nail to stop them. I'd never seen her like it! The only thing she didn't do was swear which was surprising because normally she did treat herself to the odd expletive when really riled.

The next afternoon I went to see how she was and was totally bewildered to find her restored completely. Apparently all she needed was a hefty dose of antibiotics to cure a bladder infection. Who would have thought a bladder infection could have caused such anxiety, fear, exhaustion and hilarity – and that's just in the carer.

She has been in the nursing home a week and I have to say it seems an efficient and caring place. They have nursed her back to what health she has left and fed her to her great satisfaction and been a lot more cheerful than I could ever manage. The matron is particularly cheerful and is very popular with Mother, particularly because she offers her sherry in addition to medication. I do wonder whether matron also imbibes. They tell me, with cheerful smiles, that she will be home soon. I've got mixed feelings about that. I will be pleased that it will make her happy but I have enjoyed a week's freedom and I can't say I'm looking forward to going back to the caring routine.

Once my worry over her condition had subsided I wondered where all these fantasies had come from, how extraordinary the human mind is that it can create new images and narratives from the tiniest of memories of related things. What a treasure trove of ideas are hidden in the human brain. Some people are able to turn these imaginings into wonderful books or films that in turn stimulate the imagination of others and create further memories and possibilities for them. Those authors must have found and developed a channel to release their imaginings, one which can be opened or closed at will, whereas Mother's fantasies have been released by some bacteria or other over which she has no control. It is extraordinary what magic lies dormant in my Mother's head!

***

Some time ago I did a first aid course and I only called on the training once. I was setting up sound equipment for our band's gig at a cricket club pavilion and there was a commotion from the cricket field where a game was in motion. Seeing the batsman lying on the ground, I ran out to see of I could help. He was on his back, his eyes closed, I thought he might just about be breathing. His face was smudged with soil and grass where he had hit the ground and the skin was a strange colour. I had learned that he should be put in the recovery position but the men around him would not let me touch him. They were distressed and panicking and, apart from calling an ambulance, they seemed incapable of doing anything. When the ambulance arrived they insisted it took the long route round the field to avoid damaging the pitch. The batsman was found to be dead at the scene.

When I did the first aider's course I remember one of the most frightening problems was that elderly people can bleed heavily when veins break in their legs. This morning I had to speak to the doctor again because I have noticed on Mother's legs there are pockets of red blood lying immediately under the skin, some as large as a two pence piece, others much smaller.   However, the phenomena I had observed in Mother is apparently due to prolonged use of aspirin and Mother has been on a low dose of aspirin for years having been diagnosed with angina at one time. The doctor asked the district nurse to come and take a look and now the legs are professionally dressed frequently with a protective cover in case of knocks. I rather like having the nurse come; it makes me feel a little safer and it is so much easier to ask her, in my own home, a question about Mother's

73

care rather than the more proactive solution of phoning a doctor at the surgery.

I think Mother quite enjoys visits from the lower status medical worker as it is easy to chat informerly with a nurse and not have to rise to the perceived status of the doctor. Mother's ingrained attitudes to class and gender come into their own when medical workers are involved and she has an unshakable hierarchy which she applies, which often annoys me. For example, a nurse of forty years experience has a much lower status than a newly qualified young doctor, a woman doctor is of lower status then a male doctor of the same age and a male consultant, if she can manage to identify him as such, is almost at the right hand of God.

Funnily enough Mother's attitude to doctors has been replicated several times in my work. I used to be asked to provide some role play at Manchester's teaching hospital where they examined would be consultants from all over the world. To put the candidates bed side manner to the test I was given a number of scenarios and symptoms as homework from which I improvised to give the candidates a reasonable facsimile of coping with a problem while the real consultants watched and examined.

I have had terminal illness, bereavement, bereavement through error, lost records, wrong surgery, delayed treatment and more or less anything at the NHS that could go wrong. The main skill is to make it difficult for candidates; there is no point in forgiving straight away or they have nothing to work at, and they must be able to present their expertise in patient care, which means I could really let rip with tears, anger, near collapse and threat of litigation. Such fun and useful too, as a good performance from me sorted out the sheep from the goats. Understanding how to use status often came from my observations of Mother with medical staff, although I was never as strong or as forgiving as Mother is, in role or in real life.

It always has astounded me that she has put up with so much all her life and although I have criticised her for being crabby in her old age it is really surprising she is not worse, I'm pretty sure I will be, I think I may already be. People have sometimes asked her how she has managed to live so long and she always answers 'hard work' and it may be true. Apart from having to work so hard there was always a fluctuation in our financial situation which she had to deal with.

When we were well off, and this sometimes coincided with the death of one of Max's relatives, there were new dinghies for Max, jewellery for Mother and presents for us children. One Christmas, after a magical visit to Gamages' Children's Department in their London store, my brother got a large metal Meccano set and I received an expensive doll's pram in cream and burgundy with sprung wheels and fine embroidered covers which I paraded proudly round the nearby streets with my tatty fur rabbit for a baby.

Tragedy was discovered when I returned home as I had apparently wheeled my new beauty through some dog mess which had somehow spread over the elaborate white covers and my poor furry bunny. The smell was appalling and the sparkle had definitely gone out of my new acquisition and to cap it all Mother had to wash my bunny and I wept when she pegged him on the washing line by his ears, which must have really hurt him.

When we were poor, or 'hard up' as Mother called it, there were hand-me-down clothes and only toast for tea, with jam only on the first piece, and boats, cars or projects funded during the good times were left discarded to rot. Good quality Clarke's sandals bought during plenty were worn to school without socks. Quite often at Grammar school I didn't have the right equipment and had the embarrassment of borrowing pens or being put in detention for 'forgetting' my house shoes. I never blamed Mother because I always knew she loved me and anyway I don't think this particular problem was her fault.

***

Mother ate breakfast quite well this morning and seemed brighter than yesterday. It is shower day today which always feels a bit of a marathon as shower days are the most moving she has to do. We have dressing down to a fine art now. All the bottom half, knickers, trousers, socks and slippers go on up to her knees while sitting on the bed, then the top half of vest, blouse and cardigan go on and finally she stands with the support of her walking frame while I pull the bottom half up and the top half down. But on shower days she has to hobble along the landing in her dressing gown with the walking frame and we do the undressing in a very confined space and then, what is probably the least safe operation in our routine, we have to get her over the edge of her 'walk in' shower.

Anyway here we are on this shower day and Mother is all clean and dandy and is settled into her arm chair with a rug over her knees looking out on her garden and watching the birds. I can now go upstairs and tidy the bathroom and bring down her breakfast tray.

As I come back into the kitchen Mother looks asleep, which is quite usual after the efforts made during the shower, except she doesn't look quite right, nothing in particular except just not right. I call to her and she doesn't respond. I put down the tray and touch her and call again. No response. Joe comes in having heard the panic now in my voice, he calls to her. Nothing.

Now this has happened before and although paramedics came they did not take her to hospital so this time we are in two minds whether to call 999. Last time it happened she was on the toilet and I had stepped outside the bathroom to give her some privacy but peeped in to see if she was all right. She was leaning back against the tank apparently unconscious.

I went in cautiously. It was too bizarre, too unreal, too undignified and I couldn't think what to do for a second or two. She lay at an odd angle, one which might have caused her pain in the normal run of things, and her knickers and trousers were round her ankles. Her head lay back against the wall and her false teeth had dropped from her upper jaw onto her bottom lip. Even more bizarre, now that I look back on it, was that my first instinct was to tidy her up, make her look normal, but that only lasted a split second before I called her and attempted to rouse her. I could not get any response from her. We dialled for an ambulance immediately.

She remained in that appalling state for what seemed an interminable time as we waited for someone to help, someone who would know what to do, and in the long minutes that followed she showed absolutely no sign of life apart from very light breathing. No flicker of the eye lids, no movement, nothing. I remembered a play that I had directed where the main character died on the toilet with his family knocking frantically on the locked door and the research I had done for it which indicated that it was not unusual for people to die whilst on the toilet. We wondered if she was dying and the bizarre nature of the day continued as we filled the minutes waiting for the ambulance remembering celebrities who had died on the toilet, Elvis Presley, King George the second, Catherine the Great .

I'm not sure whether I was frightened or not; there have been other times when I've wondered if this was going to be the moment but they have passed and each time they passed I got more used to riding the wave and thinking that I will definitely know when the real time comes.

The First Responder, true to his title, arrived first and was followed swiftly by two burly paramedics. In our tiny bathroom you can stand either at the basin, the toilet or the shower door, that is the total amount of space, and we now had three large men, myself and Mother, still unresponsive, on the toilet. At first they wondered if she was asleep and then they revived her with oxygen and she woke up as if nothing had happened and looked around her in astonishment and confusion. Can you imagine waking up on the toilet and seeing all those people, all those men, in there with you? Apart from obviously being very confused she looked all right. I had to clean her up and the paramedics got her back into bed and monitored her vital signs. After some while they went and we were left frightened and exhausted.

So now we feel that we might have made an unnecessary fuss and wasted the National Health Service resources so that when we find her in that same state, apparently comatose, for a second time, this time fully dressed and in her chair, we are reluctant to respond in a panic. After ten minutes or so she still is unresponsive although she does appear to be still breathing, just a barely visible movement of her chest, but her face is pallid, almost grey. It's difficult to believe it has gone on for so long, but she could just be sleeping, I could believe that at a push I suppose. But as the time goes on and my heart rate is rising she shows no sign of returning. We dialled 999 and waited.

This time, being in the kitchen where there was room to move about, the process was more orderly and less bizarre and she came round while the paramedics were doing blood pressure tests and so on and they decided to record her heart and stuck monitors all over her chest. She seemed tired but was quietly enjoying the medical intervention as she always did. The paramedics concluded that their

77

little display screen with its wobbly graphs indicated that something had happened but they weren't sure what, so they bundled her into a carry chair and off she went to the hospital.

She has been in hospital several days now and I have visited every day to find her quite well and wondering why she is there. The doctors have said the same, there appears to be no problem and I am beginning to feel rather stupid as if I have made it all up yet again. I do understand that despite the amazing advances in medical science we do not know everything, the mysteries of the human body and mind still hold many secrets, but today they have phoned to admit defeat, they do not understand what, if anything, happened and they are preparing to send her home.

Half an hour later I get another phone call from the hospital saying that while they were getting her ready to depart Mother has had 'an episode' and is currently unresponsive. This time I am not so affected with fear and confusion. I know she does this and recovers and if instead this is the time for her to go she is in 'the right place' with people who know how to handle it and have the right equipment to keep her comfortable. I tell them I will come in to the hospital to see her but when I get there she is sitting up in bed with a cup of tea and quite recovered. The staff seem apologetic that they still don't know what is wrong and I feel like saying 'Oh don't worry, I'm used to Mother leaping back from the jaws of death.'

So now she is back home, nothing has been diagnosed, she is behaving perfectly normally and maybe we will never know what happened. But these incidents, these strange happenings, add to the vulnerability of her state, they add to the fear of me being away from the house, they curtail what we can do. Can you imagine sitting in a restaurant with an unconscious old lady, unable to move her, or pushing her around a busy shop in that condition? No. Another watershed, another negative milestone in our journey together.

Chapter Seven

TRANSITIONING

I'm still taking Mother out in the car; even though the task of getting her in and out of it is so difficult and painful for her, the rides give her great pleasure and she clings to every experience, every sight and sound as if it is her last. Driving her around her own territory needs a certain amount of control over my stress levels as she is the most appalling navigator and she simply will not admit it and insists on following the map and giving directions. These directions are usually mixed in with observations about the passing wild flowers in the hedgerows or reminiscences about what happened last time she was in this vicinity. She can tell you what grows in each season on any stretch of road in a fifteen miles radius from her home but is often hazy about where the narrow lanes lead and also whether they are actually passable by car; her favourite walks of yesteryear don't always accommodate vehicles but that is forgotten if the flora is pretty.

Directions are often given with a flapping of the hand in one direction or another whilst still studying the map rather than the road and consequently an order to turn left often comes after the car has passed the turning. One of her more original commands was to turn, not by a cottage or a large tree or even a signpost but by a clump of wild garlic; you had to know your wild flowers to be navigated by Mother. She maintains that she navigated Max all through France and Switzerland some years ago but I just cannot imagine it.

Recently I managed to persuade her that I knew the way and her navigational services would not be required and we had a lovely ride out in sharp Spring weather. As we took the turn in the road towards the coast the vista opened out to show the sea stretched out in glistening sunlight with the gentle curve of the bay ending in the headland and, on left, the cliff rising, dotted with Pink Thrift, Sheep's

Bit and Sea Campion. I parked the car at one of her favourite spots and let her just drink it all in. It was so beautiful. So beautiful it overwhelmed her and made her sad and we both ended up in tears because we both knew that this beauty, which had given her the utmost pleasure through her years, now had a finite life for her. The difficulties that now accompanied every outing were forgotten and I felt I had given her a gift and I was so pleased to have done it.

The next outing was to a strange little café high on a hill which we have both enjoyed before and is fairly near home. The road leading to it, or it might even be described as a track, would surpass any pot hole campaigner's tally as the holes form an almost continuous line, but the ride is worth every bump and jolt because at the end of it the panorama across the hills is spectacular and Mother can see her little house in the distance. Its location was a blessing as it turned out because no sooner had we chosen and ordered our meal than she began to feel ill and I had to cancel the food hastily and drive her home. She went straight to bed and lay there looking pale and weak but there didn't seem to be any symptom to identify a problem.

I had a bit of a shock yesterday as Mother started to have hallucinations again but luckily I eventually recognised what was happening this time. She could hear people singing and at first I thought perhaps there was singing coming from a radio nearby as builders working on a house in the road often have the radio on, but when I looked outside there were no builders. Coming back inside I saw her joining in with the fictitious singers and nodding to me to indicate this was the song that I should recognise. By this time I was beginning to register that this was bizarre and when Mother pointed at the bedroom wall and remarked on what lovely patterns the Brownies were painting on it I knew what it was. The Brownies again; another bladder infection. I rang the surgery and they asked for a urine sample and the result came through with a prescription to sort it out. What is so extraordinary about these episodes is that they make her really happy. She enjoys them enormously and it is now one of the few times I see her smiling and laughing.

Now I am really nervous. I have tried to keep the car rides going, as I know that she would be devastated if she thought she would never again be able to go out into this countryside that she loves, but nearly every time we start out it is not long before I have to stop because she feels ill and she looks ill too. She says she feels sick and her skin breaks out in a sweat and turns so pale. On a couple of occasions I have had to stop the car at the roadside and she has had to lean out and vomit. This can't be right but I can't find anything to put my finger on that is obviously wrong. I do wonder whether she is having a panic attack, that is what it looks like and I suppose it could be a reaction to all the trauma she has gone through. I decided to leave the car rides for a while and see whether she will ask for them again. So far she hasn't.

***

Mother has had another spell in the hospital. She has been feeling sick on and off and although she still continues to eat as normal she insists on having a bowl nearby in case she vomits which so far hasn't happened. She has always had trouble with heartburn and indigestion and takes a medication which seems to keep it at bay. But one day I felt I had to call the GP as she did start to actually throw up and I could see a little blood in the vomit. In addition she seemed distressed and having severe stomach pain despite the heavy doses of drugs she was taking for her hip pain. I was a little wary that we would again be in the situation of Mother having severe symptoms at home which disappear once a medic sees her, so I kept some of the vomit, just in case, as proof.

Ridiculous I know but I am beginning to feel I am completely incompetent to deal with these medical incidents; how am I supposed to know whether they are life threatening or not? I really do wonder how I am allowed to be in charge of so many of these strong opiate drugs kept in the house without some kind of check being made. I mean I could have a go of them myself and get hooked couldn't I? I could overdose Mother if she became too irritating. Or sell them. I was once prescribed Diazepam, I seem to remember it was for anxiety, and a DJ that I knew offered to buy some from me. Just to put your mind at rest, I didn't sell them.

The GP thought she should be seen by a specialist and off we went once more in an ambulance to the hospital. We almost had to abandon the trip because as the paramedics wheeled Mother out of the door in the carry chair she screeched in pain from her shoulder and on examination they said they thought her shoulder was dislocated. They came back inside and at the same time a car started sounding its hooter outside because the ambulance was blocking the road. I went out to explain that there was an emergency and ask the driver to take another route, which resulted in an angry retort as if we had purposely messed up his day. By the time I got back inside the paramedics had apparently sorted out the shoulder problem so back to the ambulance we went and off to the hospital. This time I remembered my coat but forgot my phone.

Mother was admitted to some kind of ward where diagnosis could be done. The doctor examined her and was not able to come to a conclusion but decided to keep her in for observation.

The next day I arrived at the ward to be told they had moved Mother to another ward and the sister managed to find the location on the computer. I made my way there, waited for someone to be free, but when the nurse came she seemed confused and went away looking puzzled. Someone else came and asked Mother's name again, looked on the computer and said she's not here she has been moved to yet another ward. I went to the third ward and, once again, she wasn't there and they asked me if I was sure she had not gone home. A flash thought crossed my mind that she might be in the mortuary.

After a somewhat panicked tapping at the computer they thought they had found her and telephoned the ward to make sure before they sent me up there. I think they may have noticed I was getting a bit irritated by now, after all they had lost my Mother. Eventually I found her in the fourth ward and she seemed a little better and she had not been sick for some time, the pain had eased although she still looked ill.

Mother was in a ward with a woman who sounded as though she had dementia and who kept crying out in distress with the most bizarre utterances, all of which started with a summons for Dear Lord Jesus. The following day a nun was sitting at the woman's bedside reading from the Bible and trying to assure her that Lord Jesus was with her, so I assumed that the distressed patient was a nun. She kept her appeals to Lord Jesus going both day and night at full volume and, not only was it depriving other patients of rest and sleep, but it was very frightening. It was like a scene from a horror movie, as sometimes the ward would be quiet and then suddenly the shriek would shatter the calm and yet even in the calm you were tense as you waited for it to come again.

Several days passed, the nun had been moved, and a senior nurse took me aside and said they were not sure what was going on with Mother and the doctors didn't want to do any invasive investigation because her health was so poor. I was slightly shocked because I hadn't realised she was as poorly as that; I suppose I had got used at a very slow pace to how she presented after she came home from the cottage hospital with her broken hip. Certainly she was better now than she was then. I was told she could not be discharged until a care plan was in place; I had thought the care plan was me, but it seemed that the situation had advanced beyond my capabilities, an opinion I fully endorsed.

They kept Mother in hospital for a few days and then brought her home, with no diagnosis made, but they sent with her a bundle of notes reporting what had happened during her treatment a copy of which had been sent to her doctor. On reading through I first noticed the prescription for her medication which bore no resemblance to the one she went in with and I wondered why it had been changed since there had been no diagnosis. I read further and with rising panic wondered what it was they hadn't told me. I couldn't recognise anything about it and eventually it became so absurd that I realised these were not her notes and the treatment suggested to the GP was not meant for her. I was concerned that a GP who didn't know Mother might follow these instructions so I rang the surgery and they offered to contact the hospital to sort it out. Another disaster averted.

I totally understand how something like this could happen. Anybody going into a large hospital, even as a visitor, will see the turmoil that ensues there. There are so many people rushing about, responding to urgent situations, so much traffic of trolleys and wheelchairs, so much distress to deal with and so many diverse demands on staff. Added to that a system where every worker is on a shift pattern with only notes to pass on to explain treatment decisions, it is bound to have loopholes. The fact that my Mother's notes, amongst the thousands that were being passed from one department to another, ended up in the wrong place was not hugely

83

surprising, certainly not as surprising as losing my actual Mother in the confusion as happened at the start of this story. But the effect it had on me, after the initial shock of imagining what might have happened if she had been prescribed the wrong medication, was to throw another burden of responsibility my way. I now had to withdraw complete faith in hospitals and be vigilant about their every move.

Looking back to that first year when we arrived at her house I see how difficult she had been, how demanding and, really, how unappreciative of what we had tried to do for her, but what strength she had then as compared to now, how much control she had, how determined and vigorous she was over the things that she could still do. Now she is like a baby; she doesn't have the strength to take any control over any part of her life. She no longer objects to anything I do and is quite content to let me make all the decisions about her life, her care, what she does and when she does it.

Her lack of energy has taken her so far away from the real world and now the only world she knows is the bedroom, the kitchen and the sitting room and me and Joe and the cats. Her recovery from this last spell in hospital has been slow, she is wearing out and lacks resources to heal. It is rather like how I have been told a battery works when it gets old; every time you recharge it the energy never quite reaches full and the levels simply get lower and lower until you can't recharge any more.

I really wished they had found something wrong with Mother this time and were able to treat it because I was in a permanent state of expectation that it would all happen again. As it was she was very weak and all she wanted to do was to go to bed. There was something wrong about her, not with her physical health, although it seems nobody can decide about that, but she was different. It made me feel sad. I thought that perhaps it was her spirit that was broken.

**

Something which has emerged from the care package is that we have been offered financial help towards respite weeks. This means that Mother can go into a care home for a reduced fee for up to six weeks a year. Roz and I have visited several and got a good idea of what is available within reasonable reach of home and we have been surprised at the range of facilities. The worst was a large house whose interior smell hit us as soon as the door opened. Even from the entrance hall we could see an unkempt man in slippers and several days of beard growth leaning against the wall eating a pie in one hand. Other elderly people sat like zombies around the edges of a tatty sitting room with daytime television blaring out from one corner. All the bedrooms looked and smelt the same. I couldn't possibly leave my Mother here.

The best, and the chosen one, was clean and neat and fresh, with individual rooms whose occupants had made them their own with family photos, their choice of curtains and their own television. The dining room had tables with four chairs around to encourage conversation and in two sitting rooms, only one of which had a television, the chairs were arranged in groups around a coffee table with board games for the residents. Such simple but effective differences. The winner, however, was that sherry was always served before dinner. This was a residence for retired gentlefolk and as such the perfect place for Mother.

In some of the care homes we visited there were clients with dementia and it altered the atmosphere considerably, whereas in the home for retired gentlefolk their policy was to not accommodate dementia patients. I feel that the ethics of this are difficult to judge. If Mother had dementia and went to a home that catered for the condition I would hate to think of her ghettoised in that way and I imagine that even if you were to suffer from dementia it might be disturbing to be with others who also do. But on the other hand how can a mixed community benefit all of its members? No policy seems perfect and in addition most care homes are businesses and have to run with a profit, or at very least have to pay their staff and overheads. The absolute best place for anyone is in their own home or supported by relatives. Because it is so important to Mother it is also important to me that I shall be able to keePerhaps it is time to get more help, but I am not sure how I would use it. p her here and allow her to die in her own bed in sight of her garden.

We now have a permanent carer who comes in every morning to help Mother to wash and dress. The social worker who interviewed me at the hospital had suggested to the private care firm that we needed visits four times a day which I felt was ridiculous. What on earth would they do? Mother spent all morning in her chair in the kitchen or on the patio looking at the garden, then the afternoon mostly in bed resting and the evening in a chair watching television. A man delivered the frozen meals and all I had to do was put them in the microwave. To have someone calling four times a day would be disruptive and intrusive; I wouldn't feel I could go out. It was helpful to have someone do the washing and dressing in the morning but at night it was only a case of changing from day dress to nightie and I could still manage that.

Apparently the NHS were paying, well somebody must have been because they didn't ask me for any money and having paid privately the first time I tried carers I knew they wouldn't be offering a free service. I wondered if they thought she wasn't going to last long, something which was constantly on my mind. In the end I managed negotiate with the care company to get the service down to one carer once a day and I still don't know whether the NHS was charged for more than that. Eventually I got used to our carer and quite enjoyed her visits.

Our main carer happened to be a woman from the village whose father was a teaching colleague of Mother's and when she was not on duty we had a woman who was actually one of Mother's former pupils. It would have been too intrusive to ask but I was fascinated about how the carer felt about doing the intimate caring tasks that were involved for a person who had previously been in such a different relationship with her as her teacher. The longer I stayed in the village the more of Mother's ex-pupils I met; it seemed that most local people in their fifties had been taught by Mother and they all spoke very highly of her as their teacher. They always said she was strict but fair and I recognised how her personality worked at school as I had seen it work at home; her robust enthusiasm, her authority and her strong sense of right and wrong manifested everywhere.

Mother's cleaner, Cilla, who came on Fridays and Mother's hairdresser, Joyce, were both former pupils. Originally Mother went to Joyce's place for regular cuts and curls but now it was difficult to get her there and be comfortable so Joyce came to Mother at home. We found out that Joyce's daughter was good at manicure and it was quite a sight when they came together and Mother was sat on a chair in the kitchen with a cloth around her with one of them styling her white hair from behind and side and the other snipping, buffing and polishing her nails from the front. It was the kind of treatment Mother really appreciated, except when the nail varnish was too garish.

The first time the hairdresser came after Mother's recent hospitalisation she was visibly shocked at Mother's weakened appearance. She managed the greeting all right but as she walked round and stood at the back of Mother's chair with her scissors ready she had tears in her eyes.

***

So during the last couple of months we have settled into what feels likes a routine, a little different from what has gone before but at least it has been without major incident. Mother has her breakfast in bed and is now more patient about waiting for the carer to come and get her up, in fact she is quieter and more subdued generally. She doesn't ask to go out in the car which is a relief because while she may think it will be all right I'm pretty sure it wont be, but I don't want to have to tell her that a part of her life she has so enjoyed is probably over now.

Her friend Madge still calls now and then and it is such a welcome visit for both Mother and me because it feels as if normal life has been resumed for that short while. Madge is the only person who visits us who doesn't get paid to do so; all the others, doctor, nurse, carer, dinner delivery man are here in a professional capacity. I used to leave Mother and Madge alone to enjoy their gossip but now I have to be there because Mother has started refusing to wear her hearing aids, despite the fact that she can't always hear, and I may have to step in as re-iterator. I don't mind as I love to hear them chatting, they are both such lovely and interesting women. Madge is quite a bit younger than Mother but rather wobbly on her feet, refuses to admit it of course, but when she is ready to leave her conversation with Mother, Joe and Madge both enjoy walking together the short distance to her house. Mother used to have an abundance of friends and now most of them are dead; she is outliving them all one by one and I'm afraid there will be few if any of them left to say goodbye when Mother's time comes.

Mother has enjoyed the odd respite week at the home for retired gentlefolk although she doesn't seem to have had a great deal of social interaction. Apart from her friendship with Madge she has been shying away from meeting other people. I wonder if it is her deafness which inhibits her as she can't always hold her own in conversation now and this might make her feel a lack of the status which she has been used to. However, the food at the home is good and her independence is intact so she probably likens it to a week in a good hotel, which would definitely please her. It is also beneficial for me as I can visit my daughter for a complete break and pay attention to my relationship with Joe for a change.

Despite all her stomach problems Mother is still eating well and enjoying her food, which is a blessing as such a lot of the simple pleasures are denied to her now. Her habit of puzzle books remains and she can be heard muttering over sudoko and crosswords as she rolls through possible answers in her head. I bought her a beautiful set of colouring books featuring birds and flowers and pastoral scenes and some easy grip coloured pencils and despite finding it difficult to hold the pencils she does enjoy these pastimes but only for a short time. After a while I hear the click of the pencil being dropped onto the wooden table and a sigh, usually followed by a whispered 'I can't be bothered.' Mother was getting tired, of sudoko, of crosswords, of colouring and of life.

The amount of opiate drugs Mother is having is getting extremely worrying. I don't mean any criticism of the GPs who have been wonderful throughout, but I do wonder if there is any further she can go in terms of medication for pain relief if it is to get worse than this. She is currently on the top dose of paracetamol as well as tablets and patches of morphine and yet the pain appears to be getting worse in her hip and now has started getting bad in both her shoulder and her knee. It is really hard to hear her complaining and to feel helpless to relieve her suffering. All I can do is call the doctor yet again and say Mother is still experiencing pain despite all the medication he has already prescribed. I start every phone call with an apology because I feel that I am phoning far too often and wasting their time, but to be honest they are the only source of help I know of and they have

88

always been so kind and so supportive, so I call again and he prescribes Oramorph, the oral equivalent of the tablets and patches, to be taken when pain is very bad.

***

It's midday, twelve o'clock. I'm exhausted already. Mother is sleeping quietly now.

I took her breakfast up to her at eight and went downstairs to drink my coffee. Almost immediately there was a cry from her room, more of a groan and then whimpers. I took a deep breath and started up the stairs. Taking a deep breath turned out to be a mistake! I was less than half way up when a sickening smell of faeces crashed silently into me and forced me to alter my breathing to avoid filling my lungs with it. Once in the room I closed the door behind me to at least contain the remaining noxious gas and reached over the bed to open the window. The stench was thick in the air.

The breakfast tray had emptied onto the bed. She looked mortified, holding the duvet close against her chest. 'Oh dear...' she said in a feeble, tearful voice, 'I think I've had an accident.' I tried to assure her that it didn't matter, that it was easily sorted out, although I did not feel as confident about that as I may have sounded.

While I figured out a plan I cleared the cups and plates and picked up the bits of food from the duvet cover. I had to leave the spilt tea which was soaking through the covers. I put on some silicon gloves and tentatively lifted the duvet. It was a ghastly sight! It had spread over the bed, both under and over her in a liquid stinking mess. I knew I was going to need help. I had already injured my back trying to move her onto the commode yesterday and moving her in the bed was more difficult as it had to be done in a bending position and I was worried about attempting it, risking me getting stuck and injured further and possibly injuring her too. I didn't know how to go about it as the carers did.

I rang the central number for the care provider to see if I could get some help. There was no answer. I tried several times but it was obviously too early in the morning for anyone to be awake enough. I had no idea how I could get help. I rang 111, thinking they might know of anything available but this was obviously a request that was not in their script they didn't have an idea what I should do. I knew at least one of the carers lived in the village but I didn't know where or even whether I could ask them. I kept going upstairs to say a few words of comfort to Mother and her weak little voice telling me 'I'm all right.' made me feel even worse.

I could hardly bare it; my Mother, who had worked so hard all her life to maintain dignity and respectability, who disliked vulgarity, and who now lay patiently in her bed covered in her own excrement and I did not know what to do about it. I decided I would try the care service once more and then tackle at least the parts of the soil that I could reach. This time the manager answered and said she would send someone as soon as possible. I made a start on the easy bits.

As soon as possible turned out to be over two hours and then in breezed one young woman, probably not more than five feet tall, cheerful and confident, who dismissed my apologies for the nature of the task, refused my timid offer to assist, pulled on her blue gloves and set to work, chatting happily to Mother. A quarter of an hour later it was as if nothing had happened. The carer sat down for a cup of coffee with me and Mother was tucked up in bed as fresh and scented as a new baby. The nightmare of the last few hours was over. When someone like this diminutive carer changes the whole mood and difficulty that you, as a willing but incompetent carer, have been struggling with, the gratitude you feel is overwhelming. However this young woman became concerned about my ability to cope, in the kindest and most honest manner, and expressed her opinion that she would not be able to do what I was doing despite her youth and strength, indicating I suppose that I was far too old to be doing it.

I felt very much inclined to agree with her since I was feeling the strain on my physical body as well as on my mind. But I felt adamant that I did not want Mother to go into a home as long as I could last out. I had made considerable sacrifice to take her on and I wanted to finish the job. She had already lasted much longer than we had anticipated when we came here over four years ago and the task had been much harder than we imagined and there did not seem to be an end in sight, but we wanted to hang on. Surely it won't go on much longer; she is now ninety eight and getting weaker all the time.

Chapter Eight

DECLINE

We are in trouble again. I feel rather as if I am stuck in a revolving door because the same pattern repeats itself over and over, except this time the 'blood in the sick/ rush to hospital/ no diagnosis' has played out in a considerably more complicated manner.

Act One was familiar, the trip to the hospital in the ambulance, the waiting in the emergency department, the transition to the ward for observation and the lack of diagnosis. I do wonder increasingly whether they have an idea, for example that she has stomach cancer, but they won't tell me because there is nothing they can do about it because of her age and poor health. Perhaps they don't want to upset me, they are all very kind and gentle, but I would rather know. After all it has occurred to me that she is going to die, probably quite soon.

Act Two and we were on new territory. They decided to send her to the cottage hospital instead of coming home. Last time this happened, after Mother broke her hip, I became convinced she was about to be prescribed palliative care so I thought perhaps that was their idea, after all they probably know the signs of the beginning of death well enough and I resolved to find them for myself as soon as possible so I could make my own judgement and prepare myself.

Act Three, two weeks later, was a phone call from the cottage hospital to say would I go to the main hospital as Mother had been sent back there in severe pain and vomiting blood. At last! A doctor had actually seen what happens and I could be believed. I felt too wobbly to drive, feeling that this might be the moment when I had to say goodbye and I did not feel in the least prepared, even after all this time, and I had not yet asked Google to inform me of the signs of death, so I phoned Kit.

He drove us to the hospital, a good hour's drive away, and we located Mother in the emergency department behind the blue curtains of a cubicle. She was alone, half sitting up on the trolley, holding a paper mache bowl and looking white and shocked. She reached out a feeble, thin arm to us and said she was pleased we had come. The sight of her was frightening. I have seen her ill or in pain so many times now and of course the expression on her face and the pallor of her skin has always indicated the trauma she is feeling, but I hadn't seen her look like this before, it was different, she looked as if she hadn't enough reserves to go on. My brother looked at me and we both knew what we were thinking.

A nurse came and helped Mother to lie back more comfortably against the pillow and told us that the consultant was on his way and then she left, swishing across the blue curtain behind her. Mother had closed her eyes and you really couldn't tell if she was sleeping or unconscious. We talked in hushed whispers although there wasn't much to say. Suddenly there was quite a loud squirting noise from beneath the covers and this was followed by the most noxious smell. Mother seemed still asleep, oblivious to what her body was doing. We ran outside to find someone to help and one of the staff, without going into the cubicle, went to a cupboard and pulled out clean bedding, collected another woman on the way and they disappeared behind the curtains.

A few minutes later they emerged carrying a plastic bag and said we could go back in. I was reeling from what had just happened. For one thing I remembered that when a cat dies, and probably other animals too, they often empty their bowels as they die; I had heard it is a sign of the physical body shutting down. The other thing was the behaviour of the two nursing staff who had taken the matter over and done what must be a most unpleasant job by any standards with such calm and grace. I really admired them.

Later, with Mother still not awake, the consultant came to see her and after a few minutes he spoke to us quietly and said they were moving Mother onto a ward but he was not sure that she would survive this episode.

The next day there had been no change in Mother's condition, a waiting game had begun. I went into the side ward where they had put her, presumably to die in private, and she hardly acknowledged me. The nurse said she was not vomiting now but neither had she eaten. I sat quietly by her bed; idle chit chat was obviously not appropriate; she seemed to want to be left alone.

On the third day, as I was finishing off the housework ready to visit Mother, the phone rang and it was the consultant. He sounded enthusiastic as he introduced himself and told me he had just been to see Mother. I couldn't understand his cheerful tone of voice, I wasn't expecting it. Apparently he had walked into her ward and found her sitting up in bed chatting to the nurse and drinking tea. He said he was astonished, and pleased of course. So Mother had jumped out of the jaws of death once more and was ready to fight on.

It can't be true that an easy life with good food makes you strong, well not in Mother's case anyway. She has lived through the great depression, the second world war, had six children whilst keeping a job going, never been rich, survived cancer and a hysterectomy, known tragedy and sadness and generally had a hard life and now she defies death at age ninety eight. It must be in the genes.

After a while in the big hospital Mother was transferred to a cottage hospital set in the suburbs of a small town some distance from home. It was not at all like the last cottage hospital she resided in, more like a film set for a period drama and it was surprising not to see sisters of mercy in their bird like headdresses sweeping up the clanging metal staircases, a side ward adapted to function as the make-up room and cameras wheeling smoothly across the parquet floors. Had I been at home in Manchester I would most certainly have been ringing my independent film maker friends to tell them I had found an amazing location for a period hospital drama. But it was real, a warren of wide corridors and several large landings, uncommonly spacious for a hospital. Mother was in a huge room all by herself, whether due to lack of nurses or lack of patients I do not know.

One day while I was visiting, I think it was her second day there, the doctor, a man in his mid forties I would say, with a homely burgundy pullover under his white coat, came in to do an assessment and assured me that I did not need to leave the room. What a blessing that turned out to be! He sat some distance from the bed in a hard wooden chair with a pile of untidy papers on his lap. His opening gambit was fine and Mother was nodding in the grateful and attentive way she used for senior medical staff, although I was used

93

to her expression which said I am listening but I don't really understand what you are saying but please do continue.

I was sitting in a similar chair on the other side of the room wondering what platitudes he was going to come out with to explain the 'no diagnosis' diagnosis. After the preamble of who he was, who she was, why she was here, I heard the words 'Had your spleen removed'. My mind froze and I missed the next sentence or two before I interrupted him to ask if he had actually said those words. Unperturbed, he confirmed that he had and went on to explain convalescent treatment. I stopped him again and tried to say as diplomatically as I could that this report was incorrect and I had seen Mother every day and she couldn't possibly have had her spleen removed without my knowing. He became as confused and flustered as I was, although probably more embarrassed than I. He ran off to call the hospital and Mother became rather confused as she hadn't actually heard much of the dialogue between me and the doctor, so rather than alarm her I told her he had gone to see if she needed any particular medication.

In a situation like this who can you get cross with? Not the doctor who almost gave the wrong treatment when working from the hospital notes. Not the ward staff. Not the hospital consultant. Somewhere behind all these front-line people is a team working at passing papers or emails around with no human communication to the specialists at the beginning and end of the process. The content and significance of the messages must be meaningless to them. A typical systemic problem. Fortunately the hospital has an organised complaints system for patients and, since this is the second time Mother has been sent home with somebody else's notes with the potential to finish her off, and possibly do the same to the person whose notes they actually were, I will contact them and hope that they can spot where the system might be breaking down.

***

Mother has been back at home for a few weeks now and, although she has made what must be an extraordinary recovery, she is still very weak and managing her is more difficult. She is eating reasonably well and sleeping a lot of the time. She has not left her bed and now she has a little brass bell on the bedside table to summon me if she needs anything. She won't read or use her puzzle books and we have offered to fix up a television in her bedroom but again she has refused it. I think she is worn out, too tired for any activity. I even asked if I should get Madge to visit for a while but Mother didn't seem interested.

I think we are moving into yet another stage. I can't imagine getting her out of bed at the moment, let alone into the car, which also means there will be no breaks for respite. I feel like I now have to do everything with hardly any help from outside and it is exhausting. I'm glad Mother has the bell so that she gets help when she needs it, but the sound of that bell makes my anxiety rise at least two notches and my exhaustion follow it as I realise I have to climb the stairs yet again on my dodgy knees and aching legs.

The Spring bulbs are out in the garden but she can't lift herself up in the bed enough to see them so I have filled pots with daffodils, tulips and crocus and her windowsill, which is right by her bed, is ablaze with colour. She loves it. Last week one of the doctors paid a visit with a young student and remarked on the window sill of flowers. I said 'If Mother can't get to the garden, the garden must come to Mother.' He laughed and said to the student that she wouldn't get that in a home. Just that little remark did me the world of good. I felt justified and appreciated for a change and was glad we didn't have to put her in a home four years ago.

I was having such difficulty getting her in and out of bed to use the commode. She was able to sit up and with help could get her legs onto the floor and then stand holding on to the walking frame while we got her bottom half of her clothes down. But moving her legs to take a couple of steps to turn round to be in the right position to sit on the commode was tortuous because of the pain and lack of strength. It was so awkward with me trying to hold onto her with the walking frame in between us and then take her weight as she sat, all in an already cramped space.

It was inevitable that something would go wrong and it did, fortunately it was me who came off worse. We had only got to the part of the process where Mother stood with her legs against the bed holding onto the walking frame when she toppled first backwards and then rocked forwards and the leg of the walking frame stabbed

95

into my foot with her whole weight on it. I managed to catch her and she fell back onto the bed. The pain in my foot was excruciating; I thought I had surely broken a bone and immediately started panicking about how I could go to hospital and leave Joe to look after Mother, but the current task in hand wasn't finished so I had to wait until it was. By the time Mother was back in bed I had recovered a little and I found I could move all my toes and concluded that my bones must still be intact.

I had to make the manoeuvre easier so I phoned the social services and asked if I could borrow a turntable like the one she had in the cottage hospital and only a couple of days later they delivered one. This made it so much easier and eliminated at least some of the risk of us both falling over during the manoeuvre.

Mother has developed a pressure sore again so we have had visits from the district nurses for treatment and most of them, actually all except one of them, have been lovely people and very helpful. The exception to the norm came only once and the visit was memorable because I had what you might call a low grade argument with her. She walked into Mother's bedroom, saw the turntable, and looked at me with an accusing expression and asked me what I was doing with it. I explained, quite civilly I think, it was to get Mother from bed to commode.

I was then told I was not allowed to use it and should return it as nobody should be using equipment of that sort without training. I asked if training was available, sort of knowing that it would not be, and she replied that of course training was available, but for nurses and carers as part of their professional development. To be fair I think she caught me at a bad time because I was tired and rather overwhelmed by the increase in difficulty of my caring role but I felt so angry. I had landed with so much responsibility for decisions about caring for a very sick, possibly dying woman, to administer drugs to, to lift and move, to feed appropriately, to keep happy. I had been offered no training, I could not rest when a shift was over, I could not guarantee myself a proper night's sleep or days off, the only support I really had was the very busy GP practice who had been my lifeline through all this. In addition it had cost me money and saved Social Services, Health and Social Care a great deal. And now I am told I can't have what is essentially a piece of safety equipment because I have not had training.

I still feel angry, not because of what the nurse said so much, she simply pulled out the stopper of what I felt and let it all out, but because of all of us carers, many of whom are in a much worse situation than I am, and who receive so little recognition or support of a financial or practical or psychological nature. I would love to go to a training class with other people who find themselves in the same situation as myself.

It isn't as it used to be generations ago when the extended family shared more of the responsibility for those who had cared for them when they were small and needed protection. Whole families are seldom geographically close, women as well as men now work into retirement age to provide for the nuclear family; giving up work usually means accepting poverty at a time when extra heating and other resources are needed. We now have to rely on a nanny state that has priorities other than looking after its social services. Our National Health Service, of which we are so justly proud, is staggering at the knees from lack of prioritised funding. If I was rich I could buy a damned turntable and any other facilities or support I needed, I could even pay for training.

***

I have a feeling that Mother is not going to be able to go downstairs again. She seems to have reached a plateau in her recovery and hasn't actually been out of her bedroom since she came back from the hospital. Despite having two carers now, they are saying they wouldn't be able to get her along the corridor to the bathroom so the only moving she is doing is the transfer from bed to commode and even that is not easy to manage and is painful for her. I don't know what I will do if they say she has to use a bed pan; I can't see how I could get her onto one.

The pain in her shoulder has increased and she is having trouble with her knee. The doctor thinks it is arthritis to which she is prone anyway. I have asked her if she would like to go downstairs but she sighs as if the effort would be far too much and insists that she is all right where she is. It does make it a little more restricting for me as there is nothing else for me to do if I stay upstairs to be near her, whereas when she was in a chair downstairs I could potter around and come quickly if she needed me. If she is upstairs I also have to climb up and down the stairs more frequently. Most of the time she sleeps anyway and as I don't want to be just the potty maid or the waiter running upstairs with meals, I sit on the commode, with the lid down of course, and try to get her to talk for a while.

She sometimes asks what different members of the family are doing and although I don't keep in touch with many of them I can always tell her what my own children and grandchildren are up to and she is always proud of them as I am. Sometimes a family birthday will come up and I have asked her if she would like me to send a present and now she asks me to send some money, which of course I do, but it makes me think that before this she must have had such pleasure in thinking what we might like for our gifts and it must be many years since she actually chose a present for somebody. Being a generous person in so many ways she must miss this now I think. As a child Mother has sent me with packages of food or clothing for poor families even though we had little ourselves. When the Hungarian refugees started to arrive in this country she offered one a home. These acts must have given her so much more satisfaction than the monthly subscription to Children in Need that she makes now which goes automatically out of the bank to somebody whose story she does not know.

It is odd that Mother was so ungrateful when we first came to live with her, it was hurtful, and now she can't thank me enough. I suppose those five or so years ago she still thought she was able to look after herself, that it was just the icing on the cake to have me there, for pleasure and maybe the occasional helping hand, not as a necessity. Now there is little she can do for herself and she thanks me to the point of embarrassment on my part. Then she was still tough and sure of herself, now she asks constantly for reassurance of her worth, whether she has had a 'useful' life. I can easily respond to tell her she was a teacher; she must think of how many lives she has affected, how many seeds she has has sown which have blossomed in her pupils' lives, how many people are grateful for their time with her. She finds it easy then to turn round her mood and she usually says 'Yes. I was a good teacher wasn't I?' to which I can add the positive testimony that I hear often from her past pupils.

When she is not too tired she will add an anecdote from her vast collection of teaching tales. They are a way of self affirming that she was not always the inert old lady she has become, that once she made a very positive and useful contribution to society. The war office seconded her to wherever she was needed and she has a variety of what are now period stories from that era. She landed in a boy's school in Lincolnshire once to replace the Physical Education teacher who had recently joined up for war service and she was thrown into PE and sports throughout the school. From her description the boys seemed little short of delinquents, but she tamed them. I can imagine it. I have seen her reference when she left and it states that she was well disciplined and caring and I bet she stood no nonsense and certainly no bad manners and was every bit as strict as the man who was now fighting at the front. Whether she even knew the rules of football I have no idea but I doubt it; the only sport she participated in as far as I know was Badminton and she used to be taken to Lords by her father to watch the cricket. It's not much to go on for a whole school of hearty boys and their sporting and physical challenges. Well done Mother!

She talks about my father quite often now and it feels like sharing a very special secret that only we two know about and I suppose that is true. It feels as if she slipping past so much of her life and settling on events that are now eighty or so years ago when she was a young woman. She has so few spasmodic and fleeting memories of her time with her first husband but she stretches each moment out and cherishes them. I wonder how she must have felt when victory was declared and she saw all those scenes on the Pathe news of celebration, of dancing and singing in the streets, of throwing hats in the air, of kissing strangers, and she so newly widowed and alone. She must have clung to me, the only thing left of the past with him, the only thing left of him to take into the future, while her family and friends were welcoming home their husbands and brothers and sons who had survived the war.

I wonder what it was like for her to go about her daily life and to work and mix with a community jubilant about the victory. The propaganda of war was successful, we were all, even us children, trained to be patriotic, to hate the Germans, to swell with pride when we saw the Union Jack, to accept if not to welcome sacrifice and she must have watched the Junior boys in the playground, their arms stretched out like aeroplane wings, rat a tatting as they emulated Spitfires destroying the Gerry bombers in their glorification of the victors.

***

I've had to call the doctor as Mother seems to have deteriorated in her general health and it is difficult to get her to eat. I never in a million years thought I would ever say that! It must be serious if Mother won't eat. She is getting thin and extremely listless and when she is awake you can tell she is taking these heavy drugs. I asked the doctor whether it was all right for her to stay in bed without moving all this time and he confirmed that she was very weak and we would have to see how things went. He has prescribed some drinks for her which have all the nutrition she needs and which are very palatable so at least it may be easier to persuade her to take those. I was half expecting him to warn me that this was the last decline towards her death but he didn't; nevertheless I think it may be and neither of us was ready to form the words and let them out.

A few days ago Mother asked for some cornflakes, having not eaten for a week. She was still drinking tea and the bottles the doctor prescribed for her. She has kept asking if there is enough money, I think she means to live on, and of course there is, we don't want for anything. The only thing that concerns me just a little is the electricity bill as she complains of cold even when her room is at seventy degrees Fahrenheit and I find it oppressively hot. I monitor the heat in there and keep the electric radiator on day and night but she still says it is cold. I don't know how long this can go on. Mother says frequently that she wants to just fade away and die and it looked as though that was what was going to happen. She was frail to start off with, when she was eating, but then, well I can't believe she is going to survive not eating.

I wonder whether if I stopped looking after her she would die; if I didn't feed her, if I didn't help her to the toilet, if I didn't give her the medication, if I didn't wash her, if I just went away and didn't tell anyone. She would become incredibly distressed, she might have a heart attack, she would try to get out of bed and fall and lie for days and days until she died and nobody would know she was there. Sometimes I feel that overwhelming sudden panic I felt when I realised my responsibility as a mother of a new baby, that this vulnerable tiny creature would die if I did not care for it. It is similar with Mother but not the same. Unlike a baby she does not have to be preserved and made strong because her whole life is ahead; Mother has virtually completed her life and merely needs to be kept comfortable as the last weeks and months tick away. There is no sense of preparation, of newness, of unfolding, no forward movement. Just an endless waiting for the ticking to stop.

The doctor called again today and I was able to tell him that Mother had started taking small amounts of food, just a few spoonfuls from an ordinary dinner but it looked like it was a tremendous effort for her and she soon tired of it. It is impossible to tell what any of the doctors are thinking and I don't quite know whether to ask them if she is on the last part of the journey. I suppose they can't say that, one way or the other, perhaps they don't know and perhaps I shouldn't either. Perhaps, even, we still have a long way to go and this is quite a usual stage that doesn't necessarily ring alarm bells. I find it confusing and tiring and frightening.

Later today two nurses arrived and went to see Mother in her room from where I heard Mother telling them she was all right and how much she enjoyed the view from her window. Apart from a weakness in her voice you would not have known there was anything wrong with her. They came back to talk to me and sat together on the sofa in our sitting room opposite Mother's bedroom. They asked questions about how I was finding caring for Mother. I asked them whether we should expect Mother to ever go downstairs again because there was something wrong with the chair lift and we weren't sure what to do about it, whether it would ever be needed again. I told them about the lack of food and the wonder of her still being able to function at all and I also mentioned the recurring bladder infection, now treated with permanent antibiotics, and her strange conversations and illusions. Mother has talked a lot about death lately and how she would welcome it and she sometimes thinks she has to climb a mountain. I do wonder whether this is a metaphor

101

in some Biblical tale she has half remembered. It would fit, since she has had a life rather like struggling up a mountain and maybe she feels that by reaching the top she will achieve her Nirvana.

The two nurses left and I am still not quite sure what their assessment of Mother and me was for, except that they said they were going to accelerate her case and she would get continuing healthcare funding. I'm not sure what they meant and if it means more money I couldn't see how money would help. I have the two carers keeping Mother clean and I am managing, just about, to get her on and off the commode. A district nurse can tend to her skin on her legs and back and really there is nothing else wrong except the ongoing pain, which the doctor prescribes for. I suppose in some ways the carer service has to be a 'one size fits all' regime with just a little wriggle room for individuals. The recommended two carers four times a day doesn't work for us. We don't need it because we don't need a carer at evenly spread times throughout the day. When we did need it, the time when Mother soiled the bed, we couldn't get it. The times when Mother needs help come randomly and often at night and if carers called at times suited to them they would probably have to wake Mother from much needed sleep.

***

Today is Mother's ninety ninth birthday, another milestone survived, and despite the recent traumas and lack of food Mother is in pretty good spirits considering. I have been thinking all week about how I can make it special and I have to say I did not come up with any bright ideas. In days long gone now it was easy to choose presents that delighted her and the objects around her crowded house were testament to all the gifts she has received over many years. They range from expensive ornaments to little pin cushions or pictures crafted by the tiny hands of her children, grandchildren and great grandchildren over a period of more than seventy years. If in doubt as to what to give as her birthday present the answer was always an owl.

For some reason Mother was fond of owls and so every birthday or Christmas a new owl or owls would appear on her shelves as gifts until she had over sixty ornamental owls. There were expensive owls sitting on wooden plinths, resin owls with frightening red glass eyes, comic green owls, a lace owl in frame, glass owls, door stop owls, owl cups, owl coat hooks, soap stone owls with owl babies inside them, owls bedecked with shells and every kind of owl imaginable. Mother even named her house 'House of the Owls', but that may have been because of the owls that hooted and screeched from the barns near the house. That was before the barns were converted into desirable residences for humans and the owls were driven away.

At some point, I think it was in her late eighties, Mother called a halt to the owl presents, having really run out of house room for them, and it was about this time when she started giving away her belongings such as ornaments, jewellery, her sewing machine and so on. Despite still being able to walk up the very steep lane to the cliff and walk miles along by the sea, she made her funeral plans with Age UK. She had decided that her end was nigh and rather than expect her survivors to sort out her numerous 'objet d'art' she would present them in person to those who might appreciate them. Now, over ten years later on her ninety ninth birthday, she has surprised herself by still being here and there still seems to be no space on the shelves where all these things might have once lived.

Mother didn't want anything different for her birthday breakfast so I took up her tray with a little posy of flowers and a card from from me and Joe and two others that had arrived from family members and I had wrapped up a big box of chocolates, always acceptable whatever her circumstances. I sat on the end of the bed while she ate most of her now vastly reduced portion of the customary prunes, apricots and grapefruit and attempted to chat in as cheery a manner as I could muster.

Mother suddenly asked when her photo was going to be taken. I was confused, I wasn't sure what she meant or whether something had been arranged that I didn't know about, so I asked her which photo she was referring to. She told me that she always had her photo taken on her birthday and she appeared to be offended that I hadn't remembered this tradition. Of course I haven't been with her for every birthday of her life but I've witnessed four since we came here and I have never known the occasion to be marked photographically, but she was adamant.

The vision of several photos I had seen before flashed across my mind; they were beautiful posed, black and white, sometimes sepia images of her as a young woman, with her hair pinned and curled in the style of the thirties or forties. There were others of the same period of the three of us, Mother, my father in uniform with me as a three year old girl all sitting on a bench covered in a fluffy rug. These looked like commemorative photos, such as the soldier and his wife would keep close to them and treasure during the long separations of war time. Were these what she was thinking of from all those years ago?

I have leant that if Mother seems confused it is not a good idea to argue so I suggested that perhaps we should dress her in something pretty before we took a photo but all she would agree to was to wait until she finished her breakfast. So that is what we did and now we have a picture of ninety nine year old Mother sitting up in bed in her nightie with hardly a smile on her face. I feel like I've been in a rather bad movie with an incomprehensibly bizarre plot; it reminds me of 'Whatever Happened to Baby Jane', this very old lady wishing to have such a late birthday commemorated in this way, a less than flattering image of her for posterity.

In fact the whole day has turned out to be unsuccessful because Mother did not consider she had been given enough cards and nobody except carers visited. I hope she makes one hundred so we have a chance to redeem ourselves with a decent birthday.

Chapter Nine

BAD KARMA

The stars have aligned against us having allowed us a couple of month's respite since Mother's ninety ninth birthday. Mother started eating reasonable amounts again and whilst certainly not back to anything like acceptable vigour she has been able to chug along at a low level, sleeping between little bursts of energy she manages to muster when carers come or when I chat to her or bring drinks or meals. The Carers, are no longer able to get her to the shower so the only movement she makes is when she needs the toilet and her body is manoeuvred off the bed and onto the commode next to it with the help of the illicit turntable.

We called in a man to look at the chair lift which sometimes refused to move and he charged eighty pounds for sending it up the stairs and down again and saying there was nothing wrong. It is an ancient thing which Mother and Max bought second hand years ago and since we have been assured that Mother will not be using it again and we have no intention of using it ourselves, we dismantled it and it now stands in the garden while we find a way to dispose of it. Personally I would rather crawl up the stairs than use it. I think if Mother had not succumbed to the sales spiel she would have been walking for longer. The chair lift has been the bane of my meal deliveries to Mother upstairs as it superseded her need for a hand rail and it was such a struggle to get up the narrow stairs by squeezing past it with nothing to hold onto while carrying a tray of food or drink. So we reinstated a hand rail and bought a tray with a handle which can be managed in one hand with another hand on the rail, so my journeys up and down became so much easier.

Having removed the chair lift more of the carpet became exposed and it looked dreadful. The carpet was indented where the chair's metal support rail had been and was a different colour to the rest and

105

our darling cats had scratched several steps and even had a wee on the bottom step. It was decided, without any dispute, that the carpet had to be replaced so we started to pull it up starting from the top. We knew that the stairs had creaked and groaned for years, brother Kit being the expert as he avoided known creakers after a late night out, but we were not prepared for what we found under the carpet. It was rather like that old Flanders and Swann song where you correct one thing only to find another then another job that needs to be done.

The stairs were not built as a complete staircase in the usually known manner, in other words they did not appear to be joined to each other or to parallel side pieces the full length of the stairs; they appeared to be fixed only to the wall on each side as single steps. We could see daylight through the gaps between some of them and others had open cracks along the length of the wooden step. Honestly it looked as though the carpet and the rail of the chair lift had held them together. We called Harry the builder who said we shouldn't use the stairs until he had made them safe. He came back later that day and fixed props to hold the stairs up while a permanent solution could be arranged.

The solution was complex because Max had bricked up the original door and made an archway without a lintel under the stairs to lead to Mother's sitting room. The original door would have to be reinstated and Max's archway blocked and reinforced. It was going to be a major and very noisy building operation. Harry ordered a new staircase and we worked out with him how to mount it because it was tricky. The two walls on each side of the stairs were not parallel but the sides of the staircase would be, the gap between the walls was wider at the bottom than at the top by several inches, which would require a custom fitting to each side. At least some builders round here are used to working on these quirky ancient cottages and Harry is known to us as an arch improviser!

***

No sooner had the staircase been ordered than Mother took a turn for the worse. She became distressed and almost obsessive about her bowel movements. It has been a long battle to keep her digestive system on the go, in fact I think it might have been a lifelong concern for her. I have a feeling it is linked to her generation's emphasis on cleanliness and a possibly unreasonable expectation of the frequency with which bowels should be emptied. But of course the problem is exacerbated now because of her immobility and the constant use of pain killing drugs and it is a dance between drugs and laxatives to keep things moving.

A few days of this worry and then she plummeted back to where she was well before her birthday; she only wanted to sleep and lost all interest in eating. I think it most unlikely she will last until her one hundredth birthday, she seems so weak, at times she seems to be almost unconscious. Meanwhile the new staircase has arrived but Harry says he can store it at his house until a good time to put it in. I have no idea when a good time will be; how long can we be without a staircase while they do the job? What happens if there is no access to upstairs and Mother cries out for help? What if she dies and I can't get there? I would have to stay upstairs while the old stairs were taken out and the new staircase fitted and hope that there is no emergency for the time it takes to finish the job, and it is a job that could well come up with some more and possibly even nastier surprises.

We decide Harry will have to try cutting through the wall ready for the new doorway and we will see whether it disturbs Mother, so I go into Mother's sitting room and cover all the furniture in dust sheets. Harry starts up his grinding saw and I stay with a sleeping Mother upstairs with the door shut. The tool makes a horrendous noise but Mother's eyelids don't even flinch. At last her deafness finds an advantage!

After what seemed an age Harry finishes and we now have a hole in the wall with jagged stone around it, a house whose air is mainly stone-dust, rickety stairs held up by props with daylight shining through between the treads and a semi conscious woman. There is no way Harry can put the stairs in because he would have to work right by Mother's room and apart from the danger of being stair-less for a while I would really rather not have Mother know what is being done to her 'dear little house' because she would certainly be upset. We need to now wait and see and so we call a halt on the repairs, creep nervously up and down one side of the stairs and keep our fingers crossed.

***

Mother has been calling out at night and I have tried to rush down the narrow stairs from our attic bedroom to comfort her; sometimes she needs to be helped to do a wee and sometimes she just needs me to sit for a while and hold her hand. I'm worried about rushing down the attic stairs half asleep and disorientated in case I fall, so we have moved my bed into our sitting room opposite Mother's bedroom from where I can always hear her and get to her more easily. So now the only rooms not disturbed by inappropriate furniture or major repairs are the bathroom and kitchen.

Mother continues voicing her wish to die whenever she is awake, it is so sad, and at night when I 'tuck her in' just as she used to tuck me in all those years ago, she tells me she hopes she wont wake up in the morning. I find these conversations so difficult. I know some people deal with them by being cheery and refuting the possibility of dying, but I would just feel a sham if I did that, and in any case I sympathise with her, I would feel the same in her position and, also, I too wish she would die. This state is too much to ask of anyone, it's hideous. If I believed in God I would be praying like mad for her death. Mostly I say to her that I don't blame her for wanting to go, that maybe it won't be long now, that she is putting up with this decline really bravely and soon she will be able to rest. I feel more honest by following her lead and helping her to confront it.

I am in two minds whether to call the doctor. I don't know what else he can do. More pain killers might well finish her off. Don't think I haven't considered it! It would be so easy just to overdose her on the drugs I have in the cupboard, let her go peacefully, relieve her of this nightmare, make everything stop. I am so tempted at four o'clock of a morning and I think she would thank me for it, in fact I wonder that she hasn't asked me already. If I did do it I wonder whether anybody would know, or if they did know, would they say anything? And what if they did? What if I was found guilty and sent to prison? They would probably put me in an open prison. No more housework. No more shopping and cooking. I could read, study, paint. It doesn't sound too bad.

I wonder if Mother has thought about really trying to die; it did occur to me briefly when she stopped eating that maybe she was being proactive about ending her life. I have thought that one way to do it might be to starve, to just stop eating and drinking and to fade away. I wonder if it has crossed her mind to her to ask me to help her and whether I would be brave enough to do it. The curious thing is, nobody would blame me, in fact they would deem it an act of kindness, if it were my cat instead of my Mother.

***

After a week of bad nights we have suddenly had a good day. Mother has kept waking me up at night with odd noises or crying out. It is much easier now my bed is in our sitting room because I can make the short route while I am still half asleep and if nothing is amiss I can get back in bed without properly waking up. Usually she only needs assurance and I can sit in her room until she settles and then crawl back to my bed. The trouble is though, during the day we don't have a comfortable room to sit in now that my bed is in our sitting room and we can't both go out at the same time in case anything happens at home. Broken sleep is making me very tired and the whole house is completely depressing because of the chaos caused over the stairs and the general atmosphere of doom that hangs over us day and night.

Then I went into her room in the morning to ask if she felt like eating any breakfast and she was awake and asked me to help her to sit up. She said she had been thinking about the County Primary School, the one where she had been a teacher while I was a pupil, and did I remember Mr. Johnson. Of course I did remember because Mr. Johnson was the headmaster and it was he who took from the class of sixty children, yes, sixty, the top ten pupils, myself amongst them, to drill them for the eleven plus examination. I learnt that Mr. Johnson was famous for what the female staff called 'The Big Squeeze' which involved pretending there was not enough room to pass between the teacher and the blackboard or the teacher and the desk and thus he felt obliged to put his hands on their hips and brush himself across their bottoms. What a revelation and what a time of life for a 'Me Too' moment.

I was so pleased that Mother had really chatted for the first time for ages, but the effort of talking and listening soon wore her out and she wanted to sleep again, but what a lift the little episode had given both of us. Perhaps it only lasted minutes but even a few minutes of being happy was such a treat for us. I can't remember the last time I felt happy.

We had reminisced for quite a while about the school. In my memory it was a happy time; I liked school from start to finish. I especially loved my first teacher, Miss Greening, who taught us everything we needed to learn and played the violin for us while we copied our letters onto our chalk boards. Our classroom was heated by a huge coal fire and Miss. Greening liked to stand in front of it and lift the back of her skirt to warm her legs and at the end of each day she would say 'Hands together children' and I would put my hands together round my nose so that I could savour the intoxicating smells of chalk and plasticine as we said our evening prayer.

I never felt I was quite the same as other pupils. In the Junior and Infant school my God Mother was the head of the infant school and my Mother was a teacher in the Juniors and, as I was always in the top three in exams, other children told me it was only because of my connections and not because I was clever. Actually Mother was far too busy teaching other children to give me extra help.

The only bit I didn't like was school dinners which were taken in a brick building above the air raid shelters at the side of the playground. The puddings were the worst; usually a square lump of stodgy cake with two huge metal jugs filled with pink blancmange or unsweetened custard placed on each long table. The absolute worst pudding was tapioca or frog-spawn as we called it. My throat just closed up and refused to swallow when I felt the slimy liquid and soggy lumps. I was sick with fear because of the gigantic dinner lady standing behind me telling me I was lucky to have it and it was good for me and I had to eat it.

In Grammar school I was also something of a stranger amongst city-wise and financially secure girls from the London suburbs and I was the only naive country bumpkin from the marshes. Although I loved home and family life, it was always good to escape from the chaos of babies and clutter and unpredictability and Grammar school offered me a built in framework of rules and routines that allowed me to flourish.

Mother has been talking about Michael, one of the masters at the Junior school, and contemplating whether he was still alive. I have often wondered about Michael and whether Mother wished she had married him instead of Max. I know he was a leading light in Beachcombers and played Badminton and had a rather dull wife. Mother kept in touch with him for many years after they moved away. I also know that when I was about seven years old a man in a very smart black car pulled up outside our house when I was playing hopscotch on the pavement and enquired of me whether Mother lived here and asked me if she had ever married again after the war. He and Mother went into the front room and shut the door. I had my ear to the door the whole time but frustratingly I couldn't get even the gist of their conversation. Later I asked why he had come and Mother told me he was an old boyfriend and he had wanted to see if their friendship could be re-kindled. I always knew my Mother had lots of admirers and I could totally understand why because in my eyes she was utterly lovely. It seemed this stranger knocking on our door was offering a very comfortable lifestyle and I wished she had said yes to him because I was definitely up for an adventure of that sort.

It wasn't easy for mother to marry Max, or rather I should say that marrying him after a six week whirlwind romance accompanied by the glamour of Beachcombers Review was easy, it was the aftermath that challenged her and probably him too. To begin with it was what I call a 'mixed marriage', a term usually applied in those days to a marriage between races. In their case the mix was class. Mother was from a large respectable working class London family whose mother was a domestic worker and father a printer. Max was from a well heeled upper middle class family with military heritage and commercial success and particular conventional expectations for their son, none of which included marrying beneath his class to a woman with a child and mother was initially greeted with a stony reception. Mother modified her South London accent to a more acceptable Standard English and adopted middle class attitudes which were often at odds with a lower class income. In addition, mother had married a survivor of the war and it was

111

made quite obvious to her by local people that, since so many young men had been killed in the war there was a shortage of marriageable men, she had been selfish in taking Max. Mother liked to tell me much later on that she would have been happy to give him away at times.

But these things have a way of settling and mother found a way to jog along and cope and I think it was a similar journey for me with Max; when there is no alternative you have to cope with what there is. My relationship with Max was better in later years, partly because Max had mellowed and I had become a little more sophisticated and mature and there were increasingly areas of common ground between us.

It pleased me when I was a little older and realised that Max had the greatest respect for my father and his war service. My understanding of this helped me to begin to see him as an ally rather than a competitor to my own father. When I was an adolescent he introduced me to dinghy sailing at which he was an expert and I learned so much from him and despite him being a despot of a skipper I believe I became a competent crew. Annoying as Max could be to adults, he was a fun grand father with the little children, and everyone enjoyed his wit and humour and extensive knowledge.

Looking back without resentment I see him as a man with a wealth of unrealised talents, both physical and mental, more of Renaissance Man than Jack of all Trades, a potentially extraordinary man who never fulfilled his potential. The man he became was not the man he used to be.

The night after she had been so much better Mother woke me once again with crying out and moaning at midnight and as I entered her room I saw that she was holding her left wrist with her right hand. She was animated and looked and sounded as if she was in considerable pain. I managed to understand from her that it was her wrist causing the pain and persuaded her to let go of it so that I could see what was happening with it. The wrist was huge, swollen all round but with a particularly big lump on the front of her hand. My immediate thought was that she had broken a bone, having known from personal experience when I broke my own arm that a broken bone causes a large swelling and is extremely painful and someone as elderly as Mother could have very brittle bones. I thought she

112

must have been flaying about in bed and cracked her wrists against the wall.

I phoned 111 and a short while later a doctor rang back, suggested I use frozen peas to bring down the swelling, and said they would get a doctor to see Mother as soon as possible. I gave her a spoonful of Oramorph, which was actually due to be given in the morning, but I thought it was best to advance it as the pain seemed to be so acute. Joe had been hovering around in his dressing gown and he went downstairs to find some frozen peas and I suggested he go back to bed as there was nothing to do except wait. I wrapped the bag of frozen peas in a tea towel and fitted it round her wrist, switched on all the downstairs lights so that the doctor would see the house, and we sat to wait for the doctor to arrive.

Hours went by and I was struggling to keep awake, but as the Oramorph took hold Mother seemed to quieten down for short periods before being awoken by pain again. I found myself studying my Mother, how her body had diminished, how the skin from her arms hung down for lack of flesh to fill it, how her eyes had sunk further into their sockets, how terribly thin and frail she was, and I tried to get in my mind the pictures of her as a quite large and vigorous woman in an apron patterned with poppies beating cake mixture in a ceramic bowl, or changing a baby's nappy with safety pins in her mouth, or pushing the Silver Cross pram full of chuckling children. That was Mother so long ago and we shall never see that Mother again.

There was no change in the swelling but I noticed that sometimes her fingers flexed so I began to wonder if it really was a break or some other problem. I was worrying about what would happen when the doctor came; I couldn't imagine Mother in her present state being got into an ambulance, getting as far as the hospital and then having to have an X-ray and having her arm plastered up. I wasn't sure she would survive it. I had at last been reading about the signs of death on the internet but I could not recognise any here tonight apart from her lack of presence which might mean she was fading away; I couldn't be sure and I was frightened I might have to deal with it.

It was six o'clock in the morning by the time the doctor arrived, one of the longest nights ever. He seemed concerned the moment he came into the room and looked at Mother. He looked at the swelling

113

and didn't make a comment. He asked if Mother was getting any nursing care and I told him there was just me and the two carers who got her clean in the mornings. He made a comment about her lips being dry and that she needed nursing and I wondered if he was suggesting I had done something wrong. I have to admit I was a bit confused because Mother had been more or less like this for a while and I hadn't considered that there might be more I could do for her, that there was something missing from her care and none of the medical professionals had mentioned anything. The only new thing I had noticed was the swollen wrist. He stressed to me that I should call our GP as soon as the surgery opened in the morning, which by then was only two hours away, and I assured him that I would. On the way downstairs he asked why the house was in the state it was with a hole in the sitting room wall and the rickety stairs.

He was a perfectly sound man, I didn't think he was unsympathetic or at fault in any way, but I hadn't slept all night, I was frantic with worry about Mother and I was coping with a major building problem and as I shut the door after him I just crumpled. I sat on the bottom stair and howled, mainly in sympathy for myself. When recovered I went back upstairs and Mother asked me what the doctor had said. I couldn't really remember except that I had to call the GP so Joe and I had a cup of tea and watched the clock until eight thirty when we could call the surgery.

The GP arrived during the morning sooner than was usual for his house calls and gave Mother an examination. He looked at the swollen wrist but made no comment but when he listened to her chest he became concerned. We all went downstairs into the kitchen and the doctor asked me what was going on with the building work and I explained how the stairs had been condemned and we had made everything safe by propping up the stairs but we couldn't continue because of upsetting Mother and even as I told him I felt upset and had to try to stop myself crying. His attitude was so kind and calm and he told me I was not to worry, that I needed a break, and that he was going to arrange for Mother to go to a nursing home as he thought she had Bronchial Pneumonia. The fact that someone else was going to be found to shoulder the now increased responsibility, someone who actually knew what they were doing, was such an enormous relief that I threw my arms round the doctor's neck and thanked him probably many more times than was necessary.

The doctor explained to Mother in the gentlest tone that he wanted her to go to the nursing home where the nurses would look after her for a while and Mother took the news without any apparent alarm, although she had little strength left if she did want to object. After that he made several phone calls from our land-line, I believe to get someone on the job of finding a bed for Mother, and then he left. After all the activity had died down and Joe and I were sitting in the kitchen waiting for the ambulance I had one of those 'Oh my god' moments as I realised I was probably the first person to use frozen peas as a treatment for Bronchial pneumonia. It's just as well Mother is going to somewhere with proper nurses.

***

We were into yet another waiting game and as had happened several times already the outcome was far from certain. Time plays the weirdest tricks in these situations; sometimes dragging slowly through the minutes and then speeding up so you don't notice the minutes that have passed. It seemed an eternity before the phone rang with the news that a bed had been found for Mother in a nursing home only seven miles away, the one she had spent a week in when she had her hallucinatory period through the bladder infection. This was good news because we knew the home was a good one and we could drive there easily to visit. Then time started racing because there were things to do.

I needed to stop the carers from coming as they would be on their way soon so I phoned the main office and explained that I didn't know when or even whether they would be needed again. I suddenly realised what I had said, that I had indicated that Mother would not be coming home ever, and I didn't know whether I believed it or not. The doctor had not said in so many words that Mother was expected to die, but I couldn't quite remember what he had said. I only had a conviction that he had indicated that this was the last few days for her; I think he said something about end of life care. As I put the phone down I began for the first time to realise the significance of what had just happened, that between breakfast and elevenses we had gone from a swollen wrist to a possible last few days of Mother's life. It could be that nothing will ever be the same again for us.

We weren't quite sure what to pack for Mother's journey. We didn't know whether we were supposed to recognise that Mother might only live for a few days and pack enough for that amount of time, or whether to tactfully ignore what we had heard and pack as if she would be living normally at the nursing home and needed day wear as well as night wear, a book to read, a good supply of underclothes. It almost felt that a minimal amount might look like a prediction of her death, as if we had given up on her. In the end we tried for something in between, sort of non-committal.

Cilla arrived but it didn't seem appropriate for her to just start the cleaning as if nothing had happened so we sat down and drank tea and opened a packet of Mint Club biscuits, always a good solution to confusion. Cilla, Joe and I tried to fumble through the facts of what had happened, the expectations of what might happen and how we might cope with it all. It was as if we were in suspended animation, pretending there was a crisis when in fact all that was happening was that we three were sitting round the kitchen table drinking tea and eating biscuits while Mother was upstairs in bed, just like any normal day. We took it in turns to pop upstairs to say cheery words to Mother, who managed to open her eyes and offer a weak smile and who didn't seem to be in nearly as much pain as during the night.

At last the ambulance arrived and as I opened the door to them the paramedics looked in alarm at what they saw front of them. I tried to assure them that despite the jagged hole in the wall to their left and the way the daylight shone through the stairs it was actually safe to go up and the stairs had been well propped up from underneath. They still looked doubtful and trod carefully on their way down with Mother in the carry chair looking like a mountain rescue team on a tricky descent. Mother had no idea that the stairs did not look the same as the last time she saw them, that her chair lift was not there, and that there was a gaping hole where there used to be a wall, and I was so glad that perhaps she would never know how her 'dear little house' had creaked and groaned and been battered by the builder's saw and was in dire need of some love and attention, rather like its curator.

Chapter Ten

FROM HOME TO HOME

By the time I arrived at the nursing home Mother had already been taken up to a bedroom and the nurses were settling her in. I had to give some information to the woman in the office and I felt as if I was in a waking dream, I could hear my voice shaking and sounding far away and my legs ached almost to the point of pain. The receptionist led me up the stairs to the first floor and through a security door to a quadrangle of corridors overlooking a glass roof below and with more corridors leading off at the corners of the square. There were young women wearing coloured shirts with the home's logo on them and they came and went carrying meals to the different rooms in a quiet bustle. The corridors smelt of school dinners.

Mother is in a room at the end of one of the spur corridors in a room big enough for a hospital bed, an arm chair and side table with a small en suite room. The walls are painted cream and a window looks out over nearby gardens. There is only one picture in the room. It is a badly painted view of gondolas on the canals in Venice in a cheap wooden frame. Several phone wires pass near the window and two sparrows were swinging on them, oblivious to the human drama so close to them. Mother is lying down in the bed covered in a thin quilt and a bright knitted patchwork blanket such as volunteer knitters donate. There are alarm buttons at the head of the bed and a whirring pump for the air mattress at the foot. She is surrounded by yellowing plastic cot-sides, though Mother did not look as though she might try to climb out or fall from the edge. She was ashen faced and hardly conscious.

Two nurses in blue uniforms appeared at the doorway and while one of them came in carrying a blood pressure measuring kit the

117

other, who wore the Matron's badge, asked me to come to talk to her in the corridor. She was asking me a little about Mother and telling me about visiting and to be honest I don't think I was being very coherent. Matron put her arm round my shoulder and told me to go home and let them look after Mother. I don't suppose she had any idea how those few words felt for me. It was the most extraordinary relief, as if someone had taken away a tight iron mask from my head and I was finding it difficult to breathe as the weight lifted.

I made my way to the lift as I was afraid to use the stairs because I felt I might fall, partly because I was still walking with a stick after my foot injury and also because I felt that my legs might give way. When I got back to the reception area I asked if they would mind if I sat down and the manager led me into the back of her office to an arm chair where I sat down and burst into tears. I just cried and cried, howled like a baby, and I tried to say between sobs that what Matron had said was the kindest, most helpful thing I had heard in ages, that at last someone had offered to help me shoulder the burden of responsibility.

By this time the receptionist had made me a cup of tea and the howling subsided and the fog in my head started clearing. Of all the efficacious leaves, roots, pills and potions the infused leaf of the tea bush, taken at a timely moment, is the ultimate panacea for a multitude of ills.

***

We have had three days of waiting for Mother to die, but she continues very much the same, very subdued, hardly with us, but showing no sign of extreme illness, just extreme weakness. I sat with Mother for hours, not knowing what to say because an actual conversation was impossible, but I wanted to be there and I thought that she might feel better if I was. Carers came and went bringing tea and bedpans and I stayed for the tea but discreetly left for the bedpans.

Mother was not expected to get out of bed at all but was being expertly cared for with as little movement as possible. There were a lot of carers, all young women, all kind and polite, but it was difficult to remember each one as the shifts kept changing. I have managed to identify one who seems to be the head carer, Lizzie, older than the others and with an air of authority. She is as thin as a rake with glasses and a swinging blonde ponytail, moves very quickly like a little bird and is the only one who knows the right volume of voice to get through to Mother. I like her. She manages to be supremely polite and respectful to Mother whilst still getting the job done efficiently.

I have had to go through a bit of paperwork with the manager, who I now know is Rachel, to cover all future possibilities and make sure Mother's wishes in life or death are properly recorded. For some time Mother has carried a notice to alert medics to her wish to not be resuscitated and now we have added that it is Mother's wish to avoid going to hospital and to be left to die in peace. Of course when Mother made this wish she thought her death was to be in her own little house but I think now the wish to die is stronger than the necessity of the place, but the wish to go peacefully remains. I think if she goes here in the nursing home, as looks likely, it would be the next best thing to home.

***

A week has gone by and Mother had still not died and was beginning to look as though she has changed her mind yet again. Gradually she came back to us, a little at a time, like slowly and wearily struggling up each step of a ladder to reach at least half way to the top. Having prepared for her death we now have to revert to making her life as bearable as we can.

It is unbelievable how quickly she can recover from life threatening illness; this is now the third time I have been told to prepare myself for her demise and she has escaped the jaws of death. I am not sure she is too happy about her recovery though, I think she had a sense of relief that the end was approaching and now she has to wait in a nursing home for the inevitable to come knocking yet again. I hope it does come soon, I had so wanted her to stay at home in her little house amongst her familiar things until she died and with her garden close enough for her to say goodbye to it at the very last minute.

Mother seems to have accepted the inevitability of the nursing home graciously and is as curious as we are about how she did not manage to pass away. She is taking an interest in the food they bring her and has asked to have the television on, signs that she is picking up bits of life again having previously given in to death.

She does enjoy the inside and outside of the window. Inside the window sill is packed with plants. I have been bringing her cut flowers but they don't last long as the radiator is under the window; they die quickly. Outside she can see over people's back gardens and to the river and hills beyond. This is her outside world, sadly much diminished from her garden and the hills and cliffs and beaches that she would prefer.

I will have to get some more pictures for the room; we can always take them home again if and when she returns and there is no point in her pictures being at home and Mother staring at bare walls and studying every poor detail of the Gondolas on the canals of Venice.

We had never visited Venice although as Mother and Max got older I had taken them on holidays including several foreign trips including two to Italy. The very best of all was when just Mother and I went to Sicily after Max died. The highlight of our already wonderful trip was a visit to the restaurant at the top of Mount Etna where we sat by the window eating olives and staring at the strange alien landscape of black lava.

There was a quartet of musicians, all dark and handsome and dressed in black, red and white, playing local folk songs and pausing to serenade various diners. As they approached our table the youngest of them, playing a flute, began the first few notes of a Glen Miller song, Blue Rain, and Mother looked up in surprise. Her eyes filled with tears and as the young man leant towards her, playing just for her, the tears were falling down her cheeks. Some strange kind of kismet had made them play a sentimental song that had meant something to Mother and my father when they were apart, a song that had formed a bond across the distance between them, and whose lyrics had expressed their feelings for each other. This young, handsome Sicilian had unwittingly given her the kind of gift that could never have been planned or anticipated. As we left Sicily the next day there was smoke coming from Mount Etna and a few days later the mountain erupted and the restaurant was buried for ever under the lava.

Mother gets disorientated about exactly where the nursing home is geographically. One day she will tell me confidently where she thinks it is and get it quite wrong and the next day she has re-worked the topography and the alternative is still wrong; I have given up a detailed explanation because she forgets it, but I can understand her frustration because I always feel unsettled if I don't know where I am.

Another confusing item that is always included in our conversations is 'guess the day of the week' in which Mother states her belief that it is, say, Monday and I explain that it is Tuesday and she tries to work out why I might be right by a process of deduction such as that I had been to art class the day before or that Sunday had a different nurse on duty. I can absolutely appreciate her confusion because, apart from the influence of short term memory loss, once you retire you loose your markers such as weekends or tasks that regularly occur on certain weekdays. No such problems with the hours of the day for Mother as she had a large clock facing her bed and she calls out the time at least twice during my visits.

Mother has obviously been further weakened by this latest illness but once again there is nothing in particular that makes her so fragile. Last week the staff at the nursing home told me they had called a speech therapist to see Mother. I couldn't imagine why a speech therapist would be needed at all but apparently Mother had experienced difficulty swallowing and the therapist has given her some exercises to do to strengthen muscles. I very much doubt whether Mother will take much notice of the therapist's instructions and when I asked her about it she had forgotten that anybody had come to see her.

***

Mother is settling into the routine of the nursing home and beginning to remember certain regular events, particularly meal times. If I am there at five o'clock, and probably when I am not, she will call out 'Five o'clock! Dinner time!' like a chime on the hour, with no regard to whatever conversation we might have been engaged in. The food marks the passing of the day and Mother enjoys every meal they put before her. A chiropodist comes now and then and a hairdresser but Mother never manages to ask for them on the right day because she gets the days of the week so muddled up. To her delight two very amicable ladies come round on regular visits with a sweet trolley. Mother always minimises her dealings with the sweet trolley ladies when she reports their visits to me due to her long-standing denial of how many sweets she actually eats. She does not appear to realise that I get a bill for her sweet consumption at the end of the month. There is no point in telling her I know her naughty secret.

I can't help reflecting on how quiet Mother's life is now; these rare and short interludes with people from the real living world now bring a vibrancy that would have filled her days in times gone by. In her younger days not only was she interacting all day with colleagues and pupils in her work and stimulated by her hobbies at weekends and in the evenings, but she always had a houseful of people in addition to her large family. It seemed that additions to the eight members of our nuclear family really made no difference and so on holidays, and in particular Summer holidays, our home was filled with aunties, uncles and cousins sleeping top to toe in beds and on mattresses on the floor. Whoever and however many came Mother cared for them, fed them and made them welcome.

A particular treat was when the doctors from the United Hospitals Sailing Club were down for a week, some of them staying on our Put-you-Up sofa bed. To me they all seemed to be huge people; they could fill a room just buy being there and there were jokes and raucous laughter and teasing and sometimes, listening from my bed at night, I heard them singing 'Green grow the rushes-o' in lusty voices and haunting harmonies.

Amongst them was the first black man I ever saw. I was fascinated. I had seen pictures of black people in books but they were always dressed in grass skirts, had fuzzy hair and carried spears. But this black man was more sophisticated than any of the white men in the room, more than any man I had ever seen in fact. His features were smooth and gentle, his hands elegant with manicured nails and his voice soft when he spoke to me. I was told he was a prince and I was in total awe.

I later realised that there were more black people who lived outside of the colonial books; when I was seven or eight years old and I went to London to visit my Nana and Granddad, black people were carrying luggage on the station, conducting on the buses, cleaning the streets. It would be many more years before I saw black people with the status and sophistication of the Prince.

***

Somebody, I think it is the Health Service people, have decided that Mother is not going to die after all so we have had a 'review' with all parties concerned present. The very charming man who was acting as chair went to Mother's room to meet her and tried to explain what the meeting was about, in very general terms I am pleased to say, because if he had got into the complications of funding he might have had an extremely confusing conversation with Mother. Mother's useful contribution was to tell him that she had come in here to die but then she hadn't died and was still here, which was, after all, the crux of the whole procedure.

It was all about money really because apparently the Continuing Health Care fund she has been supported by is only for the dying and now she has decided to remain with the living. From now on, presumably until she starts dying again, she will have to contribute all of her income, that is a state pension, a teacher's pension and a small amount from her late husband's pension, but is allowed to keep twenty pounds a week for toiletries etc and eight pounds a week for 'savings'. The NHS will pay for nursing care at one hundred and fifty pounds a week and the remainder will come from Social Care through the council.

There was some talk about whether Mother was fit to go home which sent me into an absolute panic because I am still limping and using a stick from the injury to my foot that happened when I tried to move her at home and I am just recovering from back and shoulder pains too. I can't believe the authorities don't do a 'review' on the health of the carer, particularly since so many of us now are in our sixties and seventies and more and also suffering from the effects of ageing.

Anyway it was all decided amicably and it was left to me to explain to Mother which I have tried to do several times now with extremely limited success. First of all she doesn't know why she has to pay at all seeing as how we have a National Health Service that she has paid into since it started. I tried to explain that her health care was free to her, paid by the NHS but there was her food and washing and heating and so on to pay for. She did accept that, but almost finished herself off with a heart attack when I told her how much she would have to pay from her own money. I don't think she has realised the immediate implications as I have; the first that will come up will be a family birthday when the generosity of her usual presents will be affected. Mother has never been a spendthrift but she does like giving gifts and has given away around the family all of her spare money and she will not be able to do this again.

***

We haven't seen Madge for ages so I thought I had better call round and let her know where Mother was and perhaps find out whether Madge would like to go and see Mother in the nursing home. I hadn't been in Madge's house before but from the outside it is a modern detached house, built on the wild poppy field well after Mother had arrived here and quite unlike the old cottages that surround it. It was warm and comfortable inside and the sitting room had wide French windows overlooking the stream but much closer to it than other houses nearby. The walls were covered with paintings, mostly delicate watercolour landscapes or seascapes in sensitive muted colours, lovely peaceful paintings. But in the hallway were larger paintings in more vibrant colours. I asked who the artist was and it turned out that Leo, Madge's husband, was one of them and the other was their son. Leo came back from his walk while I was there and Madge asked him, almost ordered him, to make us some coffee and he disappeared into the kitchen.

While Leo was out of ear shot Madge told me he always made their dinner out of what she called a 'box' from the Co-Op which had to be microwaved and she didn't like what he chose. I gathered she meant a ready meal. Apparently Leo was an absolute stickler for

124

punctuality and all his walks, rests and meals were commanded by the clock. Nothing was allowed to interfere with his established routine. I made a mental note to observe this if I visited again as I am sure that arriving while Leo was microwaving his 'box' would throw his routine into chaos and distress him.

Leo served our coffee on a silver tray with two biscuits on a pretty plate, though how he managed to get it to us without spilling I don't know because he was even more wobbly then Madge. I complimented Leo on the paintings and he launched into a reverie about how he was an architect and had designed some complicated road system in the middle east which had never got built, and on completion of his story he abruptly left the room. Madge tutted and shook her head and rolled her eyes before telling me he had gone to his room now and he was a nuisance. I asked what he did in his room and she said she didn't know. By now I was beginning to feel I was in a theatrical farce and had lost the plot, or was it Madge and Leo who had lost it? Whichever way it was an entertaining spectacle and I thought I would like to visit them again.

***

I feel like I'm constantly having to do battle on Mother's behalf; it is more than surrogation now, it feels more like acting in her defence with public and private institutions that are not fair. In the case of the public institutions the person on the front line, the one you are obliged to deal with, is such a tiny cog in this huge unwieldy machine that all they can do is ensure that the rules and the script are followed, however sensitive they as an individual might be to the unfairness of them and I suppose the same is true to some extent of private for profit organisations. Of course something has brought this particular rant on today and opened up some previously half thought ideas into fuller focus.

I've just had a telephone conversation, for conversation read argument, with a clinic that provide diagnosis and prescriptions for dentistry, hearing and sight problems at a patient's home, or in this case the nursing home.

Mother had decided that her eyesight had deteriorated and when I suggested getting the clinic to see her she had responded with a mild refusal, the reason being she expected to die fairly soon and so it was not worth the bother. I felt that, since the only thing left to her that was easy was watching the television, it was important to do all possible to preserve her enjoyment of it and this might mean new glasses and so I persuaded her to agree to the clinic's visit. I phoned the clinic and made the appointment and was adamant that they must keep to the date and time because I needed to be there.

I had a very good reason to insist because a while ago it was suggested by the family solicitor that Mother's will had been made some years ago and she might feel she needed to update it. I talked to Mother about it and as she wanted to go ahead I tried to explain to her that since she was now 'in care' she did not have access to the kind of money she used to have and it would cost her money to change things in the will. Incidentally what she used to have was always valued by her in terms of 1950's standards, which was good in a way because she always felt well off, but at today's standards she certainly was not.

A young female solicitor came, appropriately suited up, and we talked generalities in Mother's room for a few minutes before the solicitor asked me to leave. I was very unwilling to do so because I was pretty certain that Mother was beginning to enjoy this attention and could be persuaded in any direction without my cautionary presence, but I couldn't say this in front of Mother and in any case I was aware that this was the correct protocol since I might exert pressure on Mother to my advantage. When I was invited back into the room Mother was flush with the excitement of it all, the kind attention of the young woman, the enjoyment of being asked to make her own decisions again, the satisfaction of distributing her largesse around her numerous descendants.

The new proposed will was a complete fantasy! Outside the room, as I showed the solicitor downstairs, I explained that Mother's 'estate' consisted of what the Social Care Assessment officers allowed her to keep from her pension which amounted to a few pounds a week. Essentially Mother had divided these few pounds between the large tribe of descendants so that the amount each received was so small there were no coins to manifest it, even if we still had farthings. The young solicitor's response was to insist on getting a GP to do a Mental Capacity assessment and so I had to be brutal and say that as I had Power of Attorney over both Mother's finances and her health I could assure her that Mother did not have enough money to pay her solicitor's bill, let alone an GP's assessment, and I would refuse both.

So you can see why, when I found that the clinic had allowed an optician to assess Mother in my absence I was furious. I phoned their office and complained and asked for the paperwork showing a record of the visit and the prescription to be sent directly to me. When I got it I was almost not surprised to see that Mother had spent hundreds of pounds on her new glasses.

Apart from the designer frames with varifocals she had ordered every extra and ultra and super feature they offered, including ultra-drive, and she has never learned to drive. This morning I let off steam to the company's hard worked telephonist, cancelled the prescription and then asked to speak to one of their opticians. After much insisting, and a threat to take the prescription to another optician for a second opinion, she escalated my call to some sort of senior person who eventually told me that Mother's prescription had hardly changed from her previous glasses and she could probably mange for a while on those.

These two examples both involved a vulnerable old person, Mother, and her money; fortunately I was there to stop the exploitation and in any case exploitation was not the motive for what was wrong in these two cases that were carried out by well meaning young women. But what happened and how it happened is merely magnified in the situations we read about where elderly people are robbed of thousands of pounds and I feel I can better understand how people fall into the perpetrator's trap. In these two cases with Mother the services were offered by young women who, by nature of their work, had pleasing manners, a gentle and caring approach, and professed to make the process easy to navigate with their support. They would have been hard for Mother to reject. Now move these natural, admirable qualities and place them in a salesperson with unscrupulous and devious ambition to make a great deal of easy money and the criminal fraudster is on an easy wicket.

I'm thinking that decades or maybe centuries ago our elderly folk were protected and respected by extended families. Now it is most often extremely inconvenient to care for an aged relative since

127

families are usually geographically separated and even visiting can be a disruption to the family's established life. I overheard a couple in the nursing home recently who had travelled four hundred miles to see a relative who was dying; they were her geographically nearest relatives and were hoping that her next of kin would arrive soon from Australia so that they could leave the hotel nearby and return home.

I have sometimes looked at Mother when she has been ill or when asleep and been quite shocked at her vulnerability. It is so obvious that she has no way to defend herself physically. Any body could abuse her. Anybody could rob her if she had anything to rob. Anybody could hurt her.

I have to stop myself from imagining more because it is too frightening; this old habit of mine is a potentially damaging problem caused by a lifetime as an actor, to roll out a scenario about what could happen, what one might do, what one might feel, and imagining a feeling can be very close to actually having the feeling. Of course I have played the part of someone who has done wicked things and I have wondered if I would be capable of hurting another human being or animal in real life. I think most people have wanted to hit someone but usually something stops them from moving from the thought to the action. But in some people there is something about having power over another human being or creature that breaks a boundary, opens a door that should be locked, and allows cruelty to be acceptable and even enjoyable.

There have been such horror stories of patients in institutions being mentally or physically abused and although I don't fear it in this nursing home at all I can imagine how easy it might be for my Mother to suffer it. She is at the end of a corridor, nobody would hear her shout for help especially as her voice is weak now. The carers often come into the room alone and once in there they are autonomous, they could commit any abusive act and nobody would know. They are not all sophisticated, well trained staff. Mother's protestations to other staff may not even be taken seriously as she doesn't remember well and is often confused.

But I have come to trust the staff here, particularly those who have the most contact with Mother, and although the young carers change shifts and come and go and some have more empathy than others, there is always the steadying presence of Lizzie and the

128

experience and wisdom of manager Rachel and the matron. I am so grateful to be able to trust the staff and the management of this nursing home; we were lucky to be given a bed for Mother here.

I was further grateful for the staff's wisdom recently when I felt able to take some time off and go to stay with my daughter. I received a panicked phone call from Joe because the nursing home manager had called to say that a doctor had recommended a blood transfusion for Mother. Joe couldn't remember exactly why, so I called Rachel and got the full story. Mother needed a slight change in her medication so the doctor had ordered a routine check on her blood which had come back showing an alarmingly low blood count. The obvious solution was a transfusion, but this would entail a visit to the main hospital. Fortunately Rachel had remembered that we had recorded Mother's wish to stay out of hospital and fully understood the stress and discomfort that even the journey, never mind treatment, would put on Mother. Together we decided to let Mother stay peacefully in the nursing home and risk the consequences.

***

The nursing home are really good at arranging interesting events for the patients. When Mother was in here before, during her hallucinatory period, it was her ninety eighth birthday and they got her out of bed to watch a female vocalist performing in the sitting room. It wasn't her kind of thing really and she didn't join in with the singing as some of the residents did, but near the end the carers brought in a birthday cake for her and they all sang Happy Birthday. It was such a kind thing to do and the whole event must have been stimulating for everybody.

Since Mother has been here this time there have been garden parties and singers, cake events and raffles, but Mother has been reluctant to go to any of these events and has showed no interest in engaging with other patients to the point of being anti-social. This was very different from her younger days when she welcomed all kinds of social interaction. She seems almost afraid of entering into conversation with people. It could be attributed to her deafness of course, but I don't remember her being so cautious when she was healthier; apparently she had a reputation at The Over Fifties Club for being outspoken on any occasion and always joined in activities and events. I wonder, in fact I am almost convinced, that this downgrade in her communication came when she broke her hip and became 'a disabled person', that she simply does not feel comfortable within her new persona, that she feels an acute loss of self.

The best 'event' for Mother was when they brought an owl into her room and, unlike other incidents, she did not forget it and told me several times how lovely the creature was and how she had touched its feathers. The only event I didn't like, one that gave me the shudders, was a Punch and Judy show and when I asked the desk staff why they had chosen it they said it was traditional. Well, the tradition of the original Punch way back in time in Italy was not the despicable character he became when he reached England. Punch and Judy to me is a narrative about domestic abuse, almost a celebration of wife and child beating and attacks on the police, with a comic dog thief thrown in. It is a tradition a lot of us are trying to leave behind but I suppose most of the residents are not my generation, nor the two generations that follow me, and that sort of political awareness was not part of their culture. I doubt the puppet show will produce any 'Me Too' moments from the residents.

The first of the family birthdays came up last week and I was instructed to bring Mother a chequebook. The nursing home do not like clients to have money and chequebooks around so I promised to send money instead but had to explain again that she would not be able to be as generous as before. She is finding it very difficult to take in. The same week her youngest granddaughter was going to buy her first secondary school uniform and Mother told me to pay for it all out of her money. I thought it best to comply with Mother so as not to distress her and then phoned the family to explain.

***

Mother can hardly move at all now. It is difficult to assess how she feels about it because she reveals her feelings in such a condensed and non-specific way, for example I might get there for my visit and she will say that she is 'fed up' or she might say she is

130

'bored' and yet I know that underlying these simple expressions are a host of frustrations and regrets and depression about the course her life has taken. Sometimes she will flex what she can of her fingers and simply comment that they are bent. Several times she has repeated that she is 'just lying there with her legs stretched out', the phrase repeated in the exact words each time as if rehearsed and, strangely, as if her poor legs are separate objects that do not belong to her. Several times a week she will ask me how long she is going to last. Yet in all this time, years now, she has never cried.

Thank goodness she can still feed herself even though some of the food never quite makes it as far as her mouth. Her fingers are very bent but she fits the spoon in between them in a fairly secure way and as long as the carers cut up the meat she can manage without help. It is so pathetic to watch this lady, who was so particular about table manners, propped up in bed with a plastic apron tied to her neck dropping food and spilling drinks on herself. But I think if she had to be fed by a carer I could hardly bear to watch the lack of independence and dignity.

**

I have been in absolute turmoil because I have just endured a second 'review' of Mother's situation. I had assumed that this was brought about as a matter of course as time passed but having heard what was said I now think it was simply for the Social Care department to find a cheaper way of caring for Mother. This time it was carried out by one person, whereas the first review had several case workers involved.

When I arrived at the allotted time Matron and Lizzie were already sitting round the table with the female case worker, who had already been to see Mother and I was immediately on alert because I know how gullible Mother can be and how easily manipulated she is. I was right. Mother had apparently told the case worker that she wished to go home and the meeting started from this premise. I went into panic. How could we possibly manage Mother at home? Joe and I had already expanded into the rest of the house, sure that Mother would not be returning; her little bedroom was now full of my painting stuff and desk and other hobby paraphernalia, Joe had taken over the attic as his man-cave, we had a proper bedroom at last. In any case how could we actually nurse her and move her? There certainly was no room at all for a hoist.

The case worker started talking about carers four times a day, a system which I had considered two years ago and rejected. It simply does not work in our situation; it ties us to the house, is only moderately useful and is not available exactly when you need help from other people. But she continued to explore the idea with determination until I burst into tears and became quite uncooperative and unreasonable by saying she was about to ruin my life. I think I behaved very badly but I really meant it even if I was looking like the proverbial drama queen; I didn't know how I could readjust the house, I didn't feel I could manage Mother physically, I felt totally inadequate mentally and I was so worried about keeping my relationship going with Joe having got so near the limits when Mother was at home before.

Thank goodness dear Lizzie stepped in and defended me and then the case worker moved to her plan B and started talking about a care home for Mother, the reason for this choice being transparently the financial saving for the council. By this time I believe Lizzie and matron had got the bit between their teeth and started knocking down the suggestions one by one, like coconuts off a shy, the last and winning throw being that the care home would not have a hoist and Mother could not be managed without one. It was not appropriate to hug them both but that was exactly what I wanted to do.

Afterwards I talked to matron and Lizzie about Mother being allowed to make decisions with strangers without the company of someone who knows her. It all depends upon the way in which a question is phrased. If the case worker had said something like 'Do you think you would like to go home again?' of course Mother would have said yes. But if she had said 'Do you think you and your daughter could manage at home?' she would have, reluctantly, said no, and I have been in her room on other occasions when she has admitted this to someone.

There is a sense of finality about it but I do feel relieved that it has been officially confirmed and that the nursing home staff, and especially Mother, are all in agreement. So now Mother can stay at the nursing home where the people and routines are familiar and where she has become quite content.

***

Today when I went in she was complaining about pain in her foot, this is what she does all the time, complains to me instead of complaining to someone who could remedy whatever is wrong, so I have to try to extract from her exactly what the problem is and then report it to either Lizzie or the nurse. I do hope they understand that it is not just me constantly complaining about how they are treating Mother because it seems like that to me. On this particular occasion I found that her feet were so jammed up against the wooden foot of the bed that the skin on her toes was sore and broken. I rang the bell to get help, because it takes two people to pull her further up the bed. It is such a simple thing, to wriggle yourself into a comfortable position in bed, but even that has long gone for Mother.

Some time ago when I lifted the blanket at the bottom of the bed to put her bed socks on I was shocked to see the state of her feet and legs. Her feet were pointing straight down instead of the normal right angle at the ankle and her toes were curled under her feet and the skin was absolutely white and appeared stretched over too tightly with loud blue veins on the surface. It looked so abnormal, so dysfunctional and I hadn't realised that a change like this would happen. Later I knew that it was normal for somebody who had been in bed for so long and then it became obvious that if your legs and feet are stretched out in one position for long enough they will stay there and the muscles and tendons that have stopped moving will loose their ability to do so.

Up until recently Mother has been able to have a shower occasionally by being taken from the bed in a hoist and wheeled along to a bathroom to shower in the chair. This is the only time she is ever moved, even her hair is washed in bed by Lizzie, who has developed her own skills in this task and can do it without spilling a drop of water on the bed. But the last time they got Mother into the hoist and raised up into the air she became distressed and shaky and they had to return her to the bed at once and take her pulse and blood pressure. So now the shower, of which she was so fond in her former life, is a thing of the past and all they can manage is a bed bath, her skin being wiped down by a young carer while she is pushed into the positions she can't get into under her own steam. She is extraordinarily stoic about the indignities she is obliged to suffer and it helps a lot that the carers approach their tasks with a no nonsense attitude as if bedpans and padded knickers are quite the norm.

In her proper life when she was a strong mobile woman she was rather coy, apart from her six experiences of childbirth which once started were impossible to avoid, and she did not approve of nudity at home. There was no running about half naked even as a child and there were euphemisms for all our sexual parts and bodily functions. One of the more unusual skills we had to learn was to dress and undress on the beach under a towel so nobody could see our bodies; I never quite mastered it. And now she has to endure the dreaded jade green slipper pan which has to be slid under her by one carer whilst another pushes her onto her side and she has to lie inert while they wipe her clean afterwards. I find it hard to understand firstly how she can empty her bowels in that position and secondly how she can bear it without screaming in rage and frustration.

What I do not understand though is how she is still alive when so little about her body is functioning. We are bombarded with health information that urges us to exercise vigorously for at least three half hours a week otherwise we will corrode curdle and crumble and yet Mother has lain prostrate for more than a year without doing so.

The most noticeable effect of her world collapsing into this tiny, cocooned space is in her mind. Obviously her experience of life has declined slowly with age but now it has plummeted; there is little left, nothing happens. I can't imagine what she thinks of in the long days and nights. I know she has wild dreams which frighten her and I have put that down to the drugs, but her mind functions in an odd way now. I think it worries her. She sometimes says, usually after a silence between us, that she has nothing to say and I usually reply that it doesn't matter, that I am happy to just sit with her. It is like an arrest of the mind, it goes into hibernation state and yet if I jog her memory with an anecdote from the past or even ask her if she remembers a certain incident, the electrodes fire and she comes alive again. She has lost the ability to stimulate herself so that it needs to be provided for her.

Mother has very few visitors, it is amazing how people drop off the radar so quickly, and even when family members do come she can forget the visit as quickly as a few hours after they have left. Roz phoned me one afternoon to say Mother had been upset because she hadn't seen me for such a long time, I didn't tell her I was going away and she had no idea where I had gone. I had been sitting by her bed for an hour that very morning and my immediate reaction was to feel a little angry that my visit had been so unappreciated that it had immediately been forgotten. It's no good feeling like that because it only hurts you, but it's a shame Mother gets upset when there is no need to.

Mother's lack of visitors is always compensated by her favourite visitor, Kit's dog. Kit has the most adorable and obedient young Labrador who has become a star at the nursing home; she is not the large powerful type but a svelte, lithe, little dog with a sweet character. 'Lark' knows now that the nursing home means treats, kept in a special tin by Lizzie, and cuddles from Mother. As soon as Lark enters Mother's room she is a-wagg with excitement and wants to be lifted onto the bed where she greets Mother with a pink tongued lick and settles to be petted. Lark doesn't mind if Mother is deaf and she can tolerate any amount of meaningless and oft repeated conversation, so in many ways she is an ideal visitor.

I once talked to Mother about whether she would like the traditional bench or tree to be dedicated to her memory. She was completely disinterested in the idea, she didn't want a 'place', not even a plaque in the memorial garden, she wanted her ashes thrown in the river to be taken out to sea with the tide. But when I talked to her about an idea I had that would commemorate her as a teacher, she jumped at it.

Just before her one hundredth birthday we presented a trophy in her name to the last school she had taught at. The actual trophy was commissioned from a local wood carver who made a beautiful pen nib on a plinth out of Yew. It was about eight inches tall, polished to a natural sheen with beautiful grain running through it and a brass plaque on the plinth engraved with the dedication. The trophy was to be awarded each year to a twelve year old who submitted an original piece of creative writing. There was a picture in the paper and Mother enjoyed the celebrity, even at the distance of her nursing

135

home bed, but particularly I delighted in watching her as she read through the short list from the entries, having been tasked with choosing the winner. As soon as I laid the children's papers on the bed she snapped into teacher mode; she adopted her serious face with pursed lips, and looking down her nose through her reading glasses she perused each entry with a critical eye. After due deliberation which lasted until the next day she announced the winner. It seemed appropriate and touching that she chose a sweet and loving poem written by a recently bereaved girl to her late grandmother.

***

Despite all the signs and pessimistic predictions Mother is now one hundred years and one day old. She is completely exhausted this morning after the revels of yesterday and it is hardly surprising since it takes a great deal of effort to play hostess to a large gathering when you are one hundred years old. She knew we had made preparations for a party and was looking forward to it but I think she may have been concerned, as I was, that she would not feel well enough to cope with it. Ten years ago we had a surprise party with all the tribe for her ninetieth that Kit organised at his local pub restaurant. We thought this would be the last special birthday for her. How different she was then and how astonished we would have been to know we would be celebrating yet another birthday ten years later.

Funnily enough the preparations for the one hundredth birthday celebrations began with a letter from the Department of Work and Pensions asking if Mother would like a card from the Queen. At the time Mother seemed rather disinterested and told me not to bother. Had it been Max who had become a centenarian he would have jumped at the chance to get post from Buck House. I was surprised that it had to be requested and I wondered what the reason was; could it be that republicans, or those who realised that actually it was the tax payer who paid for the card, had a hand in the option to refuse? Was this a result of austerity measures? Mother changed her mind when a man from the government department arrived to see her and then of course she seemed delighted to receive the honour.

I asked the nursing home manager Rachel if we could invite some family and have a buffet and she was more than happy to not only provide a room on Mother's floor but also a modest buffet paid for by the management. My neighbour, yet another ex-pupil of Mother's, is a semi-professional baker of celebration cakes and she offered to make the birthday cake. Kit contacted an old school chum, also one of Mother's ex-pupils, who had become the local paper's photographer, and he offered to donate his services. Because of this wonderful generosity the only thing left for us to buy was a beautiful table bouquet which the local florist made up in Mother's favourite colours with pink and mauve flowers.

We arrived well in advance of the official opening to find the the carers had decorated the party room with balloons and banners and a large cake was on the table donated by the kitchen staff at the nursing home. We added to the table the pink and mauve flower arrangement and numerous birthday cards and at the centre was the cake from our neighbour looking resplendent with a profusion of sugar flowers on top.

I had brought in a long skirt for Mother to wear as I thought this would be easy to get on her and a very expensive black velvet jacket with shiny glass buttons, and I left the carers to get Mother dressed. Meanwhile Lizzie took over running the catering in her usual efficient manner and without even being asked to and a trolley appeared, the bottom shelf loaded with sandwiches and nibbles and on top bottles of sparkling wine and tea and coffee.

Members of the tribe began to arrive, all dressed in their best, and at first the gathering took on a rather strange atmosphere as we milled around in these unfamiliar surroundings. There was nothing celebratory about the route from the front door to the patients' sitting room, it was, without doubt, a nursing home, but as more relatives arrived a subtle ownership of the room began to emerge and was well established by the time Mother could be heard being wheeled along the corridor. A huge cheer went up as she entered the room. I think she was a bit overwhelmed by how jolly the room looked with its banners and balloons and the table laden with good wishes and cakes and all her laughing and smiling descendants surrounding her.

But the best surprise came a few minutes later when her dear sister, ten years younger than her at ninety years, was guided into the room by her daughter. It was a tearful reunion. They are the last two left of their generation, from a family of two boys and four girls, and, since they are both suffering the effects of old age, it is likely this will be the last time they will be together. I am probably the only person in the room who remembers them well as young women. My aunties were adorable and all had inherited my granddad's wicked sense of humour so that staying with my Nana when the aunties were still at home was what they would call 'a scream.' There were always witty jokes, funny faces, and fooling around and always love.

Kit's friend the photographer couldn't stay too long so the first event was the taking of memorabilia. He bustled us around into various combinations from Mother with her eldest grandchild (forty-nine) and her youngest (twelve) showing the vast spread through the generations and, in contrast, Mother with the whole tribe around her showing the vast spread of all of us. After the excitement of the photograph session came the cutting of the two cakes, the one with sugar flowers from our neighbour and the one from the home's kitchen staff. Mother's hands couldn't quite manage this alone but there were many willing hands to help out.

I took it upon myself to propose a toast to Mother and just before we raised our glasses Mother realised she had downed her glass of Prosecco rather quickly and needed a refill. The hiatus was met by several bottles being proffered, the first of many refills that day. What the hell; she is a hundred years old and I did wonder whether Prosecco might be just as efficacious as opium. The feasting commenced and as we ate the relatives went in turn to sit by Mother and chat. The noise in the room began to rise as as the relaxation increased and mingling began; I'm not sure I got round to chatting to everybody. While their parents were doing their family catch-up some of the smaller children got over exited and noisy. I was a little worried in case we disturbed other patients who, after all, were in the rooms next to us and may not be feeling well, but Lizzie assured me that it wasn't a problem.

The party was well under way when I found myself sitting across the room from Mother by myself and able to take a peaceful moment just taking in the activity of the room. Mother sat with her sister beside her and when one relative moved away from them another immediately took their place, kneeling beside her wheelchair or bending towards them. Mother looked radiant. It was extraordinary when I thought about how she had looked most of the time over the past few years. Her cheeks were flushed, her eyes were bright, she was revelling in the attention and the homage being paid to her.

I am not sure how long Mother lasted out at the party; the time was so full of events and emotions that it sped by in a whirl. But eventually I saw her call me over to her chair and she admitted she was weary and wanted to get back to bed. Lizzie called two of the carers in to wheel her to her room and get her back to bed, and as she left the room there was a tremendous cheer and applause. It was a relief that everything had gone so well, particularly after the disappointment of her ninety ninth birthday, and it seems most unlikely that she will be here for her one hundred and first.

The tribe began to disperse to make their journeys, both long and short, to their homes, and it occurred to me that the next time we should all be together would be at Mother's funeral.

Chapter Eleven

SWAN SONG

The aftermath of the great birthday party has lasted well and provided Mother with memories to chew over and thoughts to ponder on as well as fresh surprises like the article that the local paper produced. Mother was pictured in her wheelchair, centre stage and smiling, looking every inch the Grande Dame, matriarch of the hoards that surrounded her. The copy below spoke reverently of her many years of service to education and various contributions to community events. Perhaps she has always enjoyed celebrity since her chosen activities have so often involved public appearances, particularly in her amateur acting days, and this week she has had eminence in abundance. So she has been supplied with her own copy of the newspaper article plus another to send to her sister, and carers arriving for their various shifts have been popping in to express their congratulations and admiration.

I went in to see Madge later and took the newspaper cutting and a report of how the birthday went. I have been to chat with Madge a few times now but I have never managed to get her in to see Mother. I arranged it twice but each time something got in the way and instead I had to take odd little gifts, a book of Cornish poetry and a paper bag of full scarves, that Madge had prepared in readiness for seeing Mother. I really must try to arrange it again, although I'm not sure how much Madge wants to go. Madge tells me that Leo is quite 'barmy' and I have to agree. If he sees me in the street he sings to me and makes theatrical gestures, or he doffs his cap in a Shakespearean bow or speaks in French. His behaviour is fine with me, I like eccentrics. But they really are 'the odd couple' because they bumble along quite well together even though to outward appearances they find each other so annoying.

Since Madge broke her leg her mobility has become affected to the extent that she cannot manage her beautiful garden and has resorted to the services of Mother's gardener Drew who calls every Thursday. I'm glad because we can't afford Drew any more although I think he is probably well in demand around the village and doesn't need us.

It is a week since Mother's birthday and she has asked me to get her a mirror. I wonder if realisation of her extreme age, celebrated so recently, had just come into focus for her. Perhaps it seemed so preposterous to her that she needed to see if this centenarian she had become was indeed the person she remembered herself to be. The idea of her looking in a mirror worries me. I don't think she had ever accepted the changes in her face when she was looking in her bathroom mirror when she was at home. I wonder if she might be shocked to see her one hundred year old face.

To cap it all she has asked me to bring in her gold powder compact with the little mirror in its lid. It has been years since I have heard mention of a 'powder compact' and even though I know the one she means, it has been even more years since I have seen it. It was round, only three or four inches across and had a raised border on the lid made out of geometric shapes and in the centre a raised gold flower with overlapping petals and as it opened it released the smell of the perfumed chalky pink powder inside.

My memory of it is me as a little girl looking upwards to observe the fascinating ritual of 'make up'. First the snap of the compact opening and her fleeting glance at the 'unmade' face, then, holding the little compact in the palm of her hand, the circular pad dabbing from compact to cheeks, a slide down each side of the nose and a final patting over the forehead, a little cloud of pink powder following the pad's journey. Next the rolling of the gold cylinder of lipstick to slowly eject the scarlet stick with its end worn at forty five degrees on one side. Balancing the compact in one hand with the lipstick in the other she would make her special face for applying lipstick in the tiny round mirror, eyes focussed down her nose, lips pulled against her teeth. The lipstick was expertly painted on in confident strokes, left to right on the top lip, right to left on the bottom. The finishing action was to roll her lips together to consolidate and spread the colour and then turn her head to the right

141

and then to the left to view the effect. I am sure Mother gave away the powder compact years ago. I circumvented the problem by suggesting a hairdresser's mirror which would give a wider view.

The 'powder compact syndrome' has become a recurring problem. Last week it was her amber necklace, before that a red book containing a collection of photographs. She always had an accurate description of where they were in the house. The necklace was in a long grey box in the second drawer down of her dressing table, the red book in a cardboard box on the left of the bottom shelf in her wardrobe, the powder compact in a wicker basket on the right of the bottom shelf of Max's kitchen dresser. The trouble was that she had forgotten that in the efforts to accommodate her hospital bed at home and all her disability equipment, the dressing table and the wardrobe had gone and were now established in my sibling's houses.

Max's kitchen dresser was worse. After the collapse of the stairs and the re-siting of the doors we had the kitchen remodelled and this included Max's dresser, but we didn't tell her in case it upset her. Max's kitchen dresser was another of his improvisations, made of the best quality timber, beautifully finished with neat dovetail joints for most of the construction, but with some very obvious uncorrected mistakes and a definite sign of boredom in the lower shelves towards the end of the build which had been covered by a curtain on a wire. It took two large men to move it and it used up the workspace on one wall. Mother loved it and because of this I couldn't throw it away and nobody else wanted it so I asked the builder to to fix the top half, which was the best bit, to the wall and use the rest to create almost matching shelves on each side. We now have the very best bits of Max's dresser above a wall-long modern worktop with cupboards below. However, there was no powder compact there before or after.

I don't think there was ever an amber necklace though there was an amber coloured glass one which didn't look cheap because the fastenings were good quality. Mother said the amber necklace cost thirty pounds and I have been puzzling ever since whether an amber necklace could, at any time in Mother's life, have cost thirty pounds. Early in her life that would have been expensive, possibly amber, later it might have been good quality glass. I wonder if Mother thinks I have sold it; surely not.

The red book remains a mystery. The more I search for it the more I think it is something she has seen in a dream, but it is upsetting her because she imagines there are precious photos in it and when I call her memory into question she feels frustrated and out of control because she can't search for it herself.

We had been in the house without her for almost a year and a lot had been changed to suit just me and Joe and our dear cats. Mother had no idea of the changes we had made and did not appear to have thought that we might want to make the house more convenient for ourselves, that we might want to use our own furniture, our own tableware and have the ornaments, pictures and precious things that signified our own past around us. In her mind everything was as she remembered it before she even took to her bed and we felt it was important that she had these memories intact because of the great love she had for her home and garden. She needed to hold them close in the strange environment she now lived in.

***

Over the months her decline has been reflected in what she is able to wear. Of course she has been unable to dress herself for some time and now and in the nursing home I wonder if she chooses her own clothes or if it is the carer's choice and if so what is their choice based on, style or convenience? I ask this because at first she was in pyjamas at night and dressed for the day. It was not long before anything below the bedclothes went and only the upper body alternated between day wear and night wear. Under cover of the covers she lay on a pad, which obviously was much easier to handle without too much movement and below the sheets the crowning glory were large fluffy bed socks in florescent yellows, pinks, or orange.

I hoped she had been able to choose her own top for day wear because Mother always liked to look what she called 'smart' and she was particular about her clothes. By this time in her life she had what I felt was a huge amount of clothes at home, two wardrobes full, some of the expensive garments bought for numerous family weddings through the years, others with labels she was rather proud of like 'Nightingales' and 'Laura Ashley'. She couldn't bear to throw

143

anything away so I rather think some of them may by now be desirable retro numbers. I once wore a colourful jacket I bought a couple of decades ago to a 'do' my acting students were having and I was asked enthusiastically where I got my retro clothes. I found it kind of heart warming that I had struck on-trend quite by accident and my fashion sense was admired by a young person.

Anyway I had brought Mother's favourite blouses and cardigans into the nursing home and folded them neatly on the wardrobe shelf where she could see them and, hopefully, choose the item she wanted to wear each day. I have been continually exasperated by the condition I find them in; rolled, creased, muddled up with socks and vests and generally dishevelled. I can't quite imagine that she is too weary to bother about this. If she had been asked to choose what to wear she would have seen the mess on the shelf and been upset by it, so I have had to conclude that rather than there being enjoyable conversation about the choice and therefore a degree of independence and respect, her top is pulled randomly from the shelf each morning and the door shut on the clothes that used to mean so much to her.

The last glimmer of pride for Mother's clothes came two weeks ago when Lizzie told me they were having such difficulty dressing her because she could not get her arms in the sleeves and that she would need all her tops to have an opening at the back like a hospital gown. I took home all her Laura Ashleys and Nightingales and even her Scottish Wool Shop jumpers and felt near to tears as I scissored up their backs and stuck crude Velcro tabs along the opening; it felt like an assassination of something that had been so very much part of my lovely Mother.

**

It has not been a good day today. Firstly I went in to see Madge and I was shocked at her appearance. She was terribly thin and weak. I felt so bad because I have been so taken up with what is happening to Mother that I hadn't called on her for ages and since I last saw her there has been an extraordinary change. I must ring her son and ask him if things are all right with Madge because I know she won't tell me herself.

144

Then I got a letter on Mother's behalf from the Department of Work and Pensions to say there had been an overpayment on her pension and she owed them sixteen hundred pounds. After I had recovered from the shock of the figure and the confusion about how it could have happened and how I could possibly get it paid back I read the letter more carefully and realised it said they would take the 'debt' from her monthly pension at a very low rate. As it is she only is allowed to keep twenty pounds a week for herself and I think it is about eight pounds for what they call 'savings' and I figured she would have to live to an unprecedented age to pay it off.

The only thing I can imagine that might have caused the overpayment is Disabled Living Allowance which she was entitled to when she lived at home and I don't know if it went on when she moved to the nursing home because her whole pension and entitlements came into her bank as one sum. Certainly I made sure I phoned the Department as soon as it became obvious that she was not going to die as predicted to let them know she had moved. There seem to be so many things like this that an ordinary person like myself, suddenly thrown out of their own familiar and well ordered life into a crisis in somebody else's life, so many unfamiliar bureaucratic systems to deal with at a time when there are also crucial humanitarian problems going on. The same systems seem to be very good at retrieving what they are owed but not so good at guiding the recipients so that mistakes are not made. I don't ever tell Mother about things like this because she always panics, especially about money.

It was with trepidation that I brought in the hairdresser's mirror for her. I knew it was a mistake but I had held out long enough and now it was time to obey my Mother and face the music. My prediction was spot on; the music was less a solo violin, more a full orchestra playing the 1812 with canon. Immediately, on the first sight of her face she gasped, and then her first words were 'I look so old!' to which I was obliged to answer 'Well you are old Mother.' She moved on to react to the lines round her eyes then the ones round her mouth, her neck, her thin cheeks and the state of her hair, each time getting more upset. I tried to comfort her with words but I don't think she heard me. I was upset too. What she had become was sitting there in the mirror next to what she used to be in both our minds and it was shocking.

Over the last few years her eyes had become smaller and sunk into her head, her skin looked transparent, her hair which used to have a soft perm styled away from her face had been cut short and straight for ease of handling, but what was really missing, as I already knew, was the sparkle of my real Mother, and she must have known, even subconsciously, that this was the biggest difference. I tried to hug her but it was awkward and all I could do was to put my face to hers and stroke her thin shoulder. For me, this limited physical contact has been difficult over these last years; a proper hug is when you put your arms round a person and hold them really close and tight. You can't hug a person properly when they are immobile in a bed or chair. It hurts me and probably her too.

***

Mother spends very little of my visits talking now and when she does the subject matter is sometimes difficult. She often talks about dying, wanting to die that is, and it is not an easy subject to respond to. I have heard people say various platitudes to her such 'Oh you're not going to die yet!' but I feel it is patronising and lacks respect to deny Mother her feelings and I try to be honest because really I don't blame her for wanting to die. I would feel the same if I were in her situation. Often she expresses deep regret that she will never see her garden again or be in her 'little house'. I always get a pang of feeling when she says this; not guilt as such because I do know that if I hadn't come here she would have been in a care home for three or four years more than she has. But her house and her garden are what she misses most and I am glad that she is not trawling over anything else in her life to regret.

On most days the conversation, if you can call it that, is frustratingly repetitive. It always consists of a short question firstly covering the weather, usually followed by asking after various family members some of whom she remembers as belonging to the wrong branch of the tribe, and, if we are lucky, we get an additional question about what I have been doing. She ponders the answers, at least I think that is what the silence is, and we start again at the beginning with the weather. Just lately she keeps asking me again if there is enough money; I always reassure her but I'm not sure whether she means to pay her bill here or for me and Joe to manage on.

It is hard to be patient, to tolerate the boredom and frustration and it sometimes makes me feel like an automaton, merely existing to give stock answers to questions with no dynamic input into our time together. I used to grumble about my duties as a carer a few years ago but they were nothing compared to this. We used to have some fun, get out and about, be able to talk and I felt I was actually making a contribution. Now my role is too passive to enjoy. During visits the time drags and to be quite honest I am sometimes glad to get away, and then I feel guilty for allowing myself to have those feelings. I think of the patience Mother always had with me whenever I was ill, how she would put me to bed and light the coal fire in the tiny iron fireplace in the bedroom and never complain about running up and down stairs with meals. She would sit with me, and read to me, and never made me feel that she didn't have time for me. And now she needs and deserves the same attention from me. I know Mother appreciates my visits and would be severely impoverished without them so I won't ever stop, I won't ever regret what I decided to do.

When she was in her sixties Mother had a hysterectomy because of cervical cancer. My sister was going for a smear test and persuaded Mother to join her, it was her first smear test at the age of sixty and it was positive. During the whole time Mother was in hospital and convalescing I was in a show and couldn't see her. Because the journey was so long it wasn't possible to get there and back in a day and it wasn't the kind of company that has understudies, I had to stay. There aren't many jobs where you are indispensable and in the big scheme of things a theatrical performance is hardly a matter of life and death, but I didn't go. I've always felt bad about it.

Sometimes she dozes, often the television is on and we both watch it. I have been introduced to so many programmes about auctions, both for antiques and houses, that I never knew existed before, I feel quite the connoisseur these days.

147

Driving home from the nursing home today I have been weighing up how much she reminisces about life when we were children. It is surprisingly little, in fact I can't remember the last time she acknowledged that part of her life. Roz says that Mother has airbrushed Max, my stepfather, out of her life and I think he's not the only one who has been given the art treatment.

It isn't that her long term memory is too poor because she remembers in great detail events and people from eighty or ninety years ago; her sisters, wartime dances in Lewisham, my father's leaves from the war front and her early work as a teacher. The one thing that animates her most is her memory of herself as a teacher. I never realised until now how important her success in her work was to her and even recently, when her conversation began to diminish, she would talk fondly about her experiences. Now we have entered a conversational world which has to be curtailed into essentials only, she will say 'I was a good teacher wasn't I?' and this is often followed by 'I have led a useful life haven't I?' The answers were not difficult to give honestly as, apart from my own good opinion of her contributions, I have so often heard unsolicited comments from her previous pupils that sing her praises.

Her short term memory is completely shot, she often thinks at eleven in the morning that she has not had her breakfast and has several times insisted that I complain to the staff who always tell me she ate heartily at nine.

Mother's social decline over the past year has been gradual but now the Mother who was always so determined and energetic despite her physical limitations has become invisible. When she came in here a year or so ago and once her health had been restored I bombarded her with choices of activity. Once she was the demon puzzler, a mistress of suduko, a champion of word search, a conqueror of the crossword, she read novels and loved to colour. Each one of these former pastimes had been weakly tried and discarded; she has not been able to summon her old self. At first she stuck to her old television viewing habits by switching on at five pm until time for sleep. Now the television is on most of the time, sometimes far too loud even though she still can't hear it and only uses the sub-titles. I think the carers switch the TVs on automatically in the mornings.

She can't be bothered to use her colouring books, puzzles require too much concentration and books are too heavy for her now crooked hands to hold up. I offered to buy a book stand for her but she seemed afraid of being obliged to make the effort to read and refused the offer. Sometimes I try to evoke her memories that until recently she loved to relate but now even that requires too much talking.

Some time ago I brought from home four of her most favourite pictures, a view of her garden that I had painted many years ago, a photo collage of some of her flowers that my daughter made her, a photograph Joe took of autumn trees near her house and a small card with a painting of jolly bell ringers. These and the clock, which was directly facing her ticking away the slow hours relentlessly, was all she had to look at when the TV was not on, and now she had nothing to occupy her mind except her chosen memories and the staff that came and went with their snatches of habitual conversation. She was becoming increasingly institutionalised.

She always likes to ask what I have been painting and sometimes I take a finished work in to show her. Once I blue-tacked a computer print of one she liked to her wall and she enjoyed having something new to look at, so I began to enlarge her collection of prints until now the wall sports more than twenty of them. In addition my grandson who travels a lot has always sent her postcards from places he visits and she wanted those pinned up too. The wall facing her bed is covered in pictures; they provide a stimulus that doesn't require any physical effort but gives her colour and action and narrative to think about. They have also taken the place of the bullocks and roses that she liked to count from her chair on the patio of her little house and everyone knows how many pictures are there and how she loves them because she tells them.

***

Mother has now passed yet another birthday, her one hundred and first. I never expected to see this one. It has been a very strange event. After the last one which was so lively and celebratory despite her frailty I was at a loss to know how to mark this one. The nursing home staff were so good; they hung banners in her room and made a cake and popped their heads round her door with cheery greetings

149

but I felt that the things I did, a card, a box of scented hand cream, a cake from Sainsburys, were all so pathetic and devoid of meaning. The one hundredth was important but this one didn't seem to be and Mother's reaction to it was careless and almost bored. Perhaps it was that her discomfort was overriding her feelings or perhaps her declining energy could no longer be mustered for any event.

***

The nurse is worried about Mother's leg, not the one with the broken hip but the good one, which has been very swollen for a few days now. They have been in touch with the doctor and now she has the leg raised on a pillow. I looked at it yesterday; both her legs look odd, this big, fat leg with the foot pointing straight down and the toes curled right under and the other leg shorter and thinner and at a strange angle with the foot also pointing down. The toes on the swollen leg look blackened or bruised to me.

There has been a change somehow in Mother's communication; still she speaks mainly in those short to the point sentences but just lately she has almost rambled. Her favourite phrase, which she now repeats often, is that she and I have spent the first six years of my life and the last six years of her life together. She loves to hear herself say this, she is happy when she says it. It makes me cry. I just hold her thin hand and stroke her hair and feel overwhelmed with emotion, with gratitude and, yes, I suppose, with love.

Sometimes it is as if she is far away somewhere ; she talked about going up a steep mountain, as she had once before, as if she was there, about having to do this difficult climb to the top. Another time she talked about her own father in the present tense, about how he was singing his music hall songs, standing with his back to the fire in his black waistcoat. She smiled and hummed faintly as she joined in with his song. She talked as if he was there, as if she could see him. And of course she talks about my father.

It is almost as if Mother has a drawer full of memories like little framed vignettes that move through a narrative. She can pull them out of the drawer and ramble about through the stories with the people she loved.

150

***

Madge has died and I didn't get round to ringing her son. I never imagined she was so ill. She has been hiding her illness from everybody and suddenly she became so weak she was taken to hospital and they were told she had very little time left to live. There was nothing that could be done, she had an advanced cancer and she was sent home to die. Poor Madge, I shall miss her. I won't tell Mother because Madge was the last friend and Mother might prefer to think she is still there.

Chapter Twelve

THE LONG FINALE

I have been to Madge's funeral at the crematorium. Madge's son gave me a lift along with his wife and Leo. When a couple have been together as long as Madge and Leo have they seem to forget the love that brought them together all those years ago, and in their old age their habits become the structure that holds their lives together. In this case it was the ready meal 'box' from the Co-Op, Leo's strict timetable for walks, rests and eating, the complaints against each other for the same annoyances year after year. I couldn't imagine how Leo would take his wife's death, even if he would know what had happened and most of the way he chatted amicably to his son, admiring the scenery and the hired car. There was a silence, and into this silence Leo suddenly dropped 'Poor old Madge. She was a good girl.'. It was such a simple utterance; so sad and so profound. It was like a window opening to reveal that love was still there.

There were only a few people at the crematorium, the members of their small family and Drew, spruced up for the occasion, Drew's wife and the chiropodist who had looked after Madge's feet on home visits. Madge had asked for a service with no religion and instead the family members read from Madge's journal. What a revelation it was. She had written this wonderful expressive journal from her early years when as a child she had given names to all the trees that surrounded her home, to the day she died and nobody had ever seen it until now.

Madge had been a farmer's daughter brought up on the Canadian prairies and later in Yorkshire. In adulthood she was an artist, had taught art, and some of the paintings she attributed to Leo and their son when I visited were hers. Madge had revealed her true self in her journal and had expressed herself through the vivid paintings in her hallway and had hidden who she really was for all these years. I felt astonished that I hadn't really known her, that I hadn't asked a question of her that would have opened this wonderful door, that I had missed so much and I couldn't understand why she had done it. Madge was a little person hiding a much larger one, presenting to the world a shadow of who she really was.

Apart from her journal there was just one reading for Madge in writing attributed to Native American Crowfoot:

'What is life? It is the little shadow which runs across the grass and loses itself in the sunset.'

I think now of Crowfoot's words and Madge when I watch the sun going down and casting long shadows on the hill that Madge and Mother used to stare at and count bullocks.

***

I'm thinking so much about dying, not me dying or Mother or Madge, just dying in general. I'm probably obsessed with dying because I keep having to face its possibility, keep preparing myself only to have to stall my emotional preparations until another day, or night.

I'm walking through the town today looking at all these people, all these hundreds of people and I'm wondering – all of them have got to die. All these hundreds of deaths. All different, unique even. And all the people, all the families that will be affected by the deaths. A woman with a baby in a sling, both to die. Two adolescents, awkward and obstinate, to die. An elderly couple walking their dog, three deaths. Who will go first and who will be left to mourn. Who will be the most capable of managing bereavement? Death pending, everywhere. All this mourning, all this disposal of goods, all these rich funeral directors.

I have noticed that it is customary when reporting a funeral to say how many people were there. 'The crematorium was half empty, such a shame'. 'It was very well attended. She would have been pleased'. Yes, life is competitive even in death. The hierarchy of popularity and reputation reaches beyond the grave. I have decided to leave my body to medical science and hope they use all my parts so that a funeral with obligatory counting of attendants becomes redundant. It's cheaper too.

So many times before I have looked at Mother and thought she can't be this ill and still be alive, but now I see the difference, her health is in a disastrous state. She is so frail, she hasn't eaten, she was vomiting for days with blood in the vomit and now is retching with nothing in her stomach. She has hardly had the strength to panic and yet panic and fear are there in her eyes and are only partially calmed by touch, by stroking her hair or holding her hand. When a person's death is announced on the television they usually describe the nature of the dying; a short illness, or a battle against cancer, nobody ever describes a long withering and shrinking, an atrophying of mind and body. Mother has no strength to 'Rage, rage against the dying of the light' as Dylan Thomas hoped to do.

She is in pain from several sources, her hip as usual, her shoulder and knee, her stomach, her toes and suddenly yesterday a sudden sharp pain in her mouth, the source of which nobody can find. Because of this pain Mother is not able to tolerate her denture and when I arrived this morning she was sitting in bed with her tray on her lap and in her hand a large piece of thick, crunchy toast they had given her for her breakfast. She had managed to tear and suck at it to get a little into her mouth but trying to eat it was distressing her and it was certainly distressing me to watch my Mother helplessly sucking at a piece of toast. I went to find Lizzie because I knew she would not have sanctioned toast for Mother's breakfast and then it was soon sorted out and replaced with mashed up fruit which Mother eat a little of, more out of duty than hunger.

Of course these things happen in an institution such as this, I understand that, and I feel for the managers who have to create order amongst a huge staff who are mostly young, all on shifts, who leave and are replaced with astonishing rapidity and most of whom do not have the wisdom that maturity brings. The managers can only set modes of practice to suit the majority of their clients, a a generic compromise, and suggest that individualism is catered for by the individual carers and especially the judgement of head carers like Lizzie. In those people who do manage to survive what is after all an extremely demanding job, the experience and understanding usually shines out. We have been so lucky to have found this place for Mother, which by all accounts that appear on television and in the press, is a beacon of good practice.

Yesterday I was sure the time had come. She had not been opening her bowels for a while and was in considerable pain. A doctor had been called on both Friday and Saturday, the out of hours doctor, or doctors, who had never seen her before. Just another aged woman in a nursing home, waiting to die.

The Saturday doctor had told the nurse on duty that if my Mother deteriorated she was to call an ambulance. So when I arrived on Sunday with Kit and his wife, the duty nurse was about to call 999, but knowing that I was on my way she had waited, getting more anxious as the minutes passed. There was a discussion bordering on an argument because I had insisted all along that Mother did not want to go to hospital to die, that the journey alone might kill her and manager Rachel had agreed with me and that decision was in clear writing on the appropriate form. I knew that at the time she had signed the form recording her wishes she had full mental capacity and I believed she had it now. I wanted a doctor to see her and if the doctor said she absolutely must go I said I would capitulate but actually I'm not sure if I would have done. I deplore the idea that hospital is the only place she is allowed to die, that she can't choose to die here in peace when they have all the facilities that might be needed. I couldn't bear the thought of her pain as they moved her in and out of the ambulance, the long bumpy journey, and then lying in a noisy ward with the bustle of strangers, the harsh light and the loneliness of dying there.

Actually, at the time I was thinking I could barricade the door of her room to stop them taking her, or, if that failed, I could remove a part of the ambulance engine to prevent it from driving as I had seen many times on the movies. That idea had to be shelved because I am ignorant about the mechanics of the combustion engine.

However this direct action was unnecessary as Rachel was called at home and agreed with me and the out of hours doctor was called. I rang my son, who has joint power of attorney with me, to discuss whether I should stick to my gut feeling and he agreed with me that we should try to keep her at the nursing home if at all possible. I wasn't entirely sure whether my power of attorney would overrule a doctor's decision but I would give it my best shot. So while we waited for the out of hours doctor to ring back I practised my speech of defiance to convince him or her to let Mother stay at the nursing home. When he phoned I began my argument in full throttle then suddenly stopped the flow as I realised he was trying to interrupt to say he agreed with me and would send a doctor as soon as possible.

The doctor turned out to be not quite a doctor but something in between a nurse and a doctor. She came into the room and sat by Mother's bed and, as is the usual protocol, she introduced herself with her name followed by her very unfamiliar title, I think it was Nurse Practitioner, and waited for Mother to respond. Mother couldn't understand who she was and probably couldn't hear her and in any case was far too ill to care who was in the room. It annoyed me because I didn't feel this was quite the time to worry about the correct protocol, this was a time for getting on with the job, so I shouted in Mother's ear that the woman was the doctor, which was sufficient to hasten the examination that was to come.

Despite my suspicions the not quite a doctor appeared to be confident and began her examinations by unsuccessfully feeling for a pulse in Mother's feet and a 'blush' at the base of the spine and evidence of noise in the bowel. She was quiet and methodical. Finally she asked us to come to a private room where we sat shakily on the empty bed looking at her like rabbits in the headlights.

It wasn't good news and the not quite doctor talked of giving Mother injections through the night until the GP could authorise the fitting of a syringe driver which would smooth her imminent passage away from this world. This was the cue for round robin text messages to the rest of the tribe. Kit undertook this task as I went to sit with Mother again and I don't know what he said but I'm sure that none of the recipients would have minded how it was expressed and would certainly not have been surprised at the news.

***

The next morning Mother's own GP came and prescribed laxatives. Laxatives! I couldn't believe it! He had first of all examined her stomach and remarked to me how bloated it was and I thought I should have realised before that her digestive tract must be

156

full, since she had been eating, even if only a little, for some time without ever having the waste products leave her body. He listened to her stomach with a stethoscope and said there was sound in there and he asked me what the observations of the not quite doctor and been on the previous day and I reported them as clearly as I could. His face gave no indication of his thoughts but he must have wondered how such a different diagnosis had been reached twenty four hours previously. I began to see the wisdom of his prescription, that he wanted to treat the pain in Mother's stomach by allowing it to empty.

The following day there was a massive evacuation and Mother felt a little better. In fact the round robin had to be repeated to say she was sitting up in bed eating prunes and watching 'The Hairy Bikers'. I swore that if we ever got the stage where a doctor issued a death certificate I would definitely be requesting a second opinion.

During the next day she appeared to stabilise in this almost optimistic condition. I say optimistic but I'm not at all sure I mean it. I think she felt better, perhaps not so frightened, but it was inevitable that it wouldn't last. How could it? And what did she have to endure before she disappeared completely? The signs of life, breathing, seeing, talking, were present but as if muted, coming from behind an invisible veil. It was tiny and frail but it was there, she was there, my Mother in every aspect, but in miniature. One of the more experienced carers, bustling into the room to change the water jug, whispered 'Brace yourself.' as she passed me.

Suddenly a nurse who I had never seen before burst in carrying a yellow bucket, rupturing the atmosphere. 'Good morning Petal!' she shrilled, 'How are we today?' There was a shocked silence which the nurse was obviously finding hard to read. I gathered, I'm not even sure how, that her yellow bucket was full of flu vaccines and she was doing the rounds of the home and bringing cheer and protection to its residents. My instinctive reaction just popped out of my mouth,

'Are you sure it's worth it?'

'Oh yes! Definitely. It spreads in places like this. You know, people going from room to room. Elderly people are...'

'No. I didn't mean...we've been told she only has a few days...'

This was not in the nurse's script. She turned to my Mother and asked her if she wanted a flu jab, resorting to the 'patient's wishes override others' mantra, and Mother, never willing to refuse free medication even at this time of her life, perked up a little, pulled up her sleeve, and was grateful.

The improvement was not to last. It was a locum GP who visited next as a result the nurse's worry about extreme pain in Mother's foot which had been swollen and discoloured for some days. He diagnosed a blood clot in her leg. He told me that if the clot moved to her lungs it would be a very unpleasant and painful death. He really did not want this to happen and was going to prescribe some blood thinning drug, that is until he got back to the surgery and read her notes. Her blood count was far too low for this to be safe; treating the blood clot could have caused her death by another means, that of a bleed. There was now a complex set of medical problems and a breakdown of systems added to her immobility. Instead a prescription for so called 'end of life' medication was given, to be used when the time came and the resident Matron and the GP had authorised its use.

I returned in the morning fairly early to find Mother more or less in the same state; hardly conscious but apparently not in pain. Instead of the usual visits from the carers and the residential nurse, the matron came to see Mother a couple times while I was there and I knew she was checking to see whether the time to use the syringe driver was near. On her third visit she spoke to me quietly to say that if there was anything I wanted to say to my Mother it would be a good idea to say it now. I thought carefully about it but really there wasn't anything to say that I had not already said many times. What would she want to hear? I think Mother knew how much I loved her and how grateful I was for how she had cared for me, for everything she had done for me. I whispered in her ear that this was the end, that she should stop striving and let go now. I have told her this before and I felt quite comfortable about saying it. I didn't want her to strive, I didn't want her to try to live. I hope she heard me.

I phoned Kit and he contacted Roz and they came over to the nursing home together to say their goodbyes. It was all so odd. How do we know what to do in these circumstances? Where in our culture is there something to refer to? Why do people cover these weird times with euphemisms instead of sharing what it is like to die or to watch someone you love die so that those following them have some knowledge that might help? We three siblings ended up talking to each other in an unconfident, stagnant and engineered way, even talking about other people's illnesses, which seemed so irrelevant compared to what we were witnessing at this very moment, the death, the very last moments of our Mother.

Since there was no progress towards Mother's death, Kit and Roz went back to their homes and to carry on their lives and I stayed on wondering what I should do; stay here in case she died soon or go home to rest a little in case it takes a long time and I need to be here later on. I couldn't make up my mind, I kept going through each alternative and trying to work out the consequences of a decision and how each might make me feel. Matron came back into the room. The time had come at last and the syringe driver was inserted in her thigh. There is no going back now. She is going to die this time.

***

I'm writing this with a 2B pencil in an almost dark room and it is exactly midnight. It is the room where Mother is dying. I've put the light on in the en suite as it doesn't shine in her eyes but it gives me just enough light to write. The reason why I've got the 2B pencil is that I'm sitting with her through the night because I don't want her to die alone and I thought I might be able to sketch to stop my mind churning relentlessly. I can't sketch. I can't concentrate.

I went home earlier in the evening. I was advised to have a rest. I wouldn't have gone at all except Lizzie offered to sit with Mother. I knew she was actually on duty and I didn't think it would be fair to her but she said she would only be doing her paper work so she could sit in Mother's room and do it. So I thought I felt all right about leaving Mother and perhaps it was a good idea to rest and relax a bit in case whatever it was I was about to face went on for a long time, I could perhaps stop thinking about it and get engrossed in watching TV at home with Joe. Well, easier said than done. I told myself it was fine, I had a cup of tea and tried to settle down in front of the television but as I watched Barnaby tackle the third murder in Midsomer Norton and there was obviously still at least one more dead body to come, my mind was still in her room and I imagined her crying out for me, so I came back here.

I've tried watching the television in her room and managed most of 'My 600 pound Life' but mostly I've been listening to her breathing. I've heard people say you have a certain number of breaths in your life. These will be her last few. I wonder how many. If I knew how many I would know when she will die. This afternoon her breath kept stopping and starting again but now it's more even.

This afternoon was so different to this strange night I am enduring. She could hear me this afternoon, at least I think she could. I leant very close to her ear and said who I was and that I was going to stay with her and there was a tiny movement in the muscles around her eyes in response. I think, I hope, that she wanted to tell me it was all right, that she was ready to go, that she was simply waiting for nature to take it's slow but sure course. She wouldn't know of course that nature was being aided by prescription drugs.

There was still some life then, in her and in the building. The shift was changing and one of her carers popped her head round the door to say goodnight to me. As the building quietened I could hear Dorothy from two doors down the corridor. Dorothy doesn't need to have people to talk to; she's quite happy talking to herself. Tonight Dorothy has been upset by a corned beef sandwich delivered to her at tea time and is venting her anger to an empty room.

'The food! The sandwiches! Bloody sandwiches. They don't care. It's bloody poison! I'll spit it all out if I can. I'm not gonna put up with this, of course I'm not. I'm telling everybody, they should know. What can I do? I'm not hurting anyone. Bloody scarecrows in the bathroom! I'll bloody drown myself. I've never had this, never, never, never. It's not right for a woman of my age.'

Poor Dorothy, as if she hasn't got enough to worry about, being bedridden in a nursing home, without having a fear of being poisoned. The carers are so kind to her; they know she is not just a patient, Dorothy is somebody's Mother too.

The night shift is quite different to the day shift. There's electric light everywhere. There's no bustle, no girls giggling or speaking in loud, high pitched carer's voices. Just two televisions blaring out in the next corridor; a musical competing with a war film. The building is stark, too bright, devoid of humanity. I don't know the night staff. I wish Lizzie was on duty.

There's a fly in the room. I'm so angry with it. How dare it come near my Mother when she's dying. It's landed on her face. This is unbearable, I feel such overwhelming hatred for this fly and I can't swat it with her puzzle book because the noise might disturb her. This fly is disturbing her peace, it isn't right; they don't have flies intruding like this in the movies.

***

I've read everything Google has to offer on the subject of death. I want to know everything. That way I won't be shocked. I am clued up on Cheyne stokes breathing, she will stop breathing for a few seconds and then start again. This is a sure sign that death is on its way. Then there is the Death Rattle, another sure sign. This I have seen on the movies. I have a black and white image etched on my mind. This is how it goes:

The scene opens: the elderly relative lies in a large bed, propped up by well stuffed pillows. The family, already racked by grief, surround the bed, supporting each other and taking civilised turns to whisper their individual and fond goodbyes and place their gentle kisses on the pale forehead. With no precipitence at all the soon to be deceased patriarch makes a reasonably inoffensive guttural rattle and lays his head to one side. A soft whimper, the epitome of pathos, can be heard from one of the women and gentle, not too loud, crying comes from another. It is now time for one of the ubiquitous platitudes to cover the death scene and the camera moves in for a close up on the eldest son who says 'Well, he had a good innings.' End of scene. This is known as 'a good death'. I wonder if this one will be.

***

I am here in her dying room for a second night. It is not at all like in the movies.

The death rattle is noisy and sustained and it has been going on for six hours already. The sound reminds me of making jam; that crucial moment when the hot jam is bubbling and popping and you mustn't stop stirring or it will stick to the bottom of the pan. Except

161

this sound is rhythmic, the breath being heaved in through mucus and forced out, in and out, in and out and then suddenly changing to a terrifying screech and whine, then back to its hideous choking rhythm again. A little while ago the nurse came in and gave Mother an injection and the sound quietened but it came back with more insistence and filled the room again.

She is not responsive now and I'm not sure that she can hear me any more, but she has not gone, she is still here. Even when the women come to change her pad and move her almost dead weight she does not respond. When they go I slip my hand under the covers to feel her fingers. They are cold but further up her arm is warm. She is still here. I lean towards her ear to tell her that I will wait, that I love her, that she can let go now, that she has done enough, that it's nearly over. Perhaps she can still hear me.

The noise is so loud I can hardly bear it. I wonder if I could walk round the corridors that surround the four sides of the quadrangle. I tell her I'm just going to take a short walk, just a little break. In the first corridor the sound of the death rattle fades, in the second and third I can't hear it, in the fourth it approaches and reaches full volume as I turn in the door. Nothing has changed. I can't leave the room for too long in case something does change.

I try to snuggle down into the arm chair, on my side and facing her, and pull the thin blanket the nurse has given me up to my chin. I close my eyes and the tired muscles around them feel the relief but there is no chance of sleep, I am wide awake inside. There are only two things moving in the room now; my breath and hers. There are only two sounds in the room; the gentle insistent ticking of the clock and the rough insistent death rattle. Everything else is silent and still.

And then something changes. Following an outward rattling breath I hear two little clicks – and then nothing. I sit up suddenly and look at her, waiting for the next intake of breath. I wait and I wait. It doesn't come. Her face is draining, she is leaving, quietly and peacefully she slips away like a piece of beautiful white silk draping and sliding over and away from this poor old body. And then nothing, no presence, nothing. She has gone.

I am not in the least bit nervous or panicked. I feel as if everything has gone quiet and peaceful and a heavy cloak has sipped away from my back. Quite methodically I press the call bell and go to wait by the door and in moments I hear the footsteps of the carer hurrying towards me. I tell her that Mother has gone and there is a short silence between us. The carer said that the nurse would need to 'do his checks' and asked if I wanted a moment alone with Mother before he came. I didn't need to. Mother was not there.

I realised that the nurse would need to be sure Mother was actually dead and I sensed there was some urgency about it. I remembered that matron had said something last afternoon about getting her moved as quickly as possible. I presume that a body starts to deteriorate quickly in a warm place. I have suddenly thought of the American TV drama, CSI, and one of the characters is Grisham who is the entomologist, who can always tell how long a body has been dead by the insects that are present to invade the body. I thought of the obscene fly that arrived earlier to worry Mother; was it the first responder, arriving too early?

Epilogue

ASHES TO ASHES

It is two weeks since the funeral. I do not have the sense of closure that these rituals are intended to give the bereaved, I don't even know if I needed it. I don't have a sense of being bereaved even. I looked it up in the dictionary to check and I don't think I feel it. Perhaps there is something wrong with me, perhaps I am unlike others. Perhaps I have been too busy to think about how I feel; I've just been doing what has to be done. This is the first time I have stopped to look back.

It has been seven years, seven years out of my life; sad, irritating, boring, difficult years. Years full of extreme love and extreme frustration. It is no comfort to think that there are people worse off than myself; to think that just makes me feel guilty. I have felt part of a community I have never met, whose lives have been taken over by the needs of someone they love. I don't know who they are or where they are but I acknowledge them with humility. I only know that we share something that is only known by us.

My daughter helped me to empty Mother's room at the nursing home. I was worried about doing it. I thought it might upset me. But as we entered the room it was just an empty room, with the bed not made up and the now rather tatty pictures on the wall. The room where so much anxiety and sadness had seeped into the walls was just a drab room, a dead room. The pictures that had meant so much to her had lost their reason for existence; it wasn't difficult to take them down and discard them into a bin bag. We went through her things and there was so little there; colouring books and puzzle books she hadn't touch for months, boxes of hearing aid batteries, her butchered clothes now not fit even to pass on to a charity shop. I felt no attachment to any of it, nothing was significant, nothing I could treasure as a memory of Mother.

Sometimes now when I do think about Mother I think she is still in the nursing home and I have to correct myself to remember she is dead. I went to shop at Morrison's and automatically headed straight for the plants to buy one for Mother. Recently I had to drive to the town where she has been in the nursing home and I almost turned into the street as I had done so many times over the last year or so. Having got over the shock of my instinct kicking in like that, I felt a lonely, hollow feeling in my chest and almost had to convince myself she wasn't there. Perhaps that is what bereavement means. I am sure that if she had died at home I would miss her more; her room would be empty, every piece of the house would feel different, my ears would be alert for a sound from her room, her presence would be missed every minute.

I wrote to all the pension people the day after Mother died to let them know and two of them, having said their condolences very briefly, informed me that Mother had been overpaid and they would be requiring a repayment. Sweet of them.

I had to collect Mother's ashes on Friday. There were forms to sign, I suppose to make a record of who had taken Mother into custody, and they handed me an ornate royal blue bag which, in turn, held a royal blue box, the type of box in which one might receive an expensive gift. So this was all that was left of my Mother. I was completely at a loss as to how I should feel and found myself watching and waiting for something to emerge. I was doing that actor thing, listening to myself to discover how I felt, watching for the manifestation of my grief and I found that I was not moved by the strange days I have travelled through and I wondered if I should be.

When I got home the only place I could think of putting the ashes was in the cupboard with my paints and canvases and for the next few days I kept testing myself to see if Mother in the cupboard would upset me. She didn't seem to. I had expected to hear from her in some way. I am quite sensitive to the spirit world usually; I see my deceased cats in my peripheral vision, I felt my sister sitting next to me in the car, my granddad stood at the foot of my bed and said goodbye, I sense Max standing by the coffee maker, and in our house in Manchester, Mrs. Green, the woman who died there before we moved in became quite a regular with her observation of us. All of them have been welcome visitors. But I can't find Mother anywhere,

165

I even walk down her garden and listen for her but she doesn't speak to me. She is nowhere to be found, except in my head and in this story.

I have heard about other people's decisions as to where to keep their loved one's ashes, all of them bizarre. One kept on the mantelpiece in the sitting room, another in the shed, another always placed as a centrepiece on the dinner table. Our Mancunian friend in New Orleans asked his wife to put some of his in the Mississippi, some in The Netherlands where they had both lived for a while and the rest in his beloved home town of Manchester. They were carried across the three country's customs borders in a rum bottle.

I have sorted through the objects that were part of her life and I feel a strong sense of being the custodian of things that she loved. I think she would be pleased that some of her descendants that she loved so much will wear her rings, that some of her is imprinted in the gold and silver and will become part of them, that others will pass by an ornamental plate on their wall and think of her. Most important of all is that Joe and I will be custodians of her little house and precious garden and although I will never be a gardener of her calibre I will honour the years of work she put into making this special place.

***

Today I have had a revelation which has disturbed me. I was in the Chemist shop buying a new toothbrush and stuck to the counter was a leaflet about pain relief which I read once quickly and then wondered if I had misunderstood so I read it for a second time. At the top of the page were a series of boxes labelled with various pain killing drugs and one of them I took particular notice of because it said Morphine, the drug Mother had taken ever since she broke her hip and the dose of which had been steadily increased as the pain apparently kept troubling her.

Mother had eventually graduated to having six paracetamol a day, a Morphine patch and in addition a liquid Morphine, Oramorph, and she still complained of pain. I was finding it difficult to believe she could still feel pain and wondered if some of her problem was psychological, but even the Matron at the nursing home was surprised in those last few days when Mother flinched at the needle when given an injection. The leaflet on the chemist's counter indicated that the effect of Morphine wears off and it is not even certain that it is 100% effective anyway. All this time I have been thinking that Mother has been getting worse and worse when, in fact, I now can believe that it was the drugs getting less and less effective.

I was so angry partly because I didn't know that pain killers might not work, I thought you could move up the scale and when you got to morphine nothing could hurt. Why on earth did I not look on the internet? That was my first port of call for everything else, but it didn't occur to me to check this one. I have grown up with the idea that I can put my trust in doctors, I thought that whatever the pain there would be a drug for it, for any illness there would be a cure and the body would cut out pain messages to the brain if it became unbearable. So when Matron saw Mother flinch at the injection she was right; even in her very last hours Mother felt it, and I now feel extremely guilty about doubting her.

So now I realise that something I have never really been afraid of, I do have to fear. The flesh is very weak, the older you get the more you realise that human beings are not infallible. I once saw on television the effect of a car hitting a water melon, the melon being similar in density to human flesh. On impact the melon dispersed in a cloud of small pieces. It was a stunning demonstration of the vulnerability of human flesh. Evolution has been so extraordinarily clever but has left some extraordinary weakness too. Our minds have developed with such complexity that we are able to create many ways to save ourselves and our planet and we have created even more that will destroy both.

***

I don't think I will ever want to 'do' Christmas again. It has never been a religious event for me because of my disillusionment with the Church but when children and grand children were around it was about giving them happy memories of a traditional festival. Most of my adult life Christmas has been about working in pantomimes or children's shows or functions with the band and these last few years have been dominated by disturbing events.

Several have been pathetic attempts to make a Christmas for Mother, either at home with putting up her decorations and serving a Turkey ready meal, with no guests, sentimental television programmes and very little cheer. Once we went to Roz for Christmas dinner and it was a disaster. I had to load up walkers, wheel chair and commode as well as Mother into my small Ford Fiesta and then unload it all on a busy road with no pavement outside Roz's house.

There was no room for Mother's chair in the dining room so we ate one of Roz's superbly cooked meals on our laps in the front room and then half way through Mother became desperate to use the commode which we had put in the dining room. I tried to continue eating but it wasn't easy as I could hear Roz getting stressed as she tried to get Mother onto the commode. It seemed she was only partially successful and Roz was obliged to spend most of her mealtime trying to save her soiled dining room carpet. It is extraordinary how much effort it takes to deal with this kind of situation and we were all exhausted afterwards.

One of the things I loved about Madge was her aversion to Christmas. She resented it as much as I did and was quite vocal in her hostility towards the practice of it. Her Christmas cards were put in an unhappy pile on the cupboard, pictures facing down. It isn't only the adoption of the mid-Winter festivals which have adapted so badly to religious uses. The worst thing it brings out is the greed of corporates who pretend it is all about good will and cause so much in the way of expectation which often ends in debt and misery.

In the nursing home they always made a wonderful effort for Christmas and there was decoration, music and festive meals for everyone including visitors. For Mother's first Christmas I had a sombre meal sitting in a chair in her room and the second year Mother was moved to the common sitting room to eat in company with me and other people. Sharing our table was a severely disabled woman suffering from Multiple Sclerosis who needed to be fed by the carer. Firstly it is difficult to watch a relatively young woman tolerating this indignity and I felt so sad for her that life had dealt her such a bad card.

More crucial for me personally was that my beloved sister's life had been ruined by this disease and she had had to go in residential care while her dear children were still young and she had died at the age of thirty five. The meal was agony for me as the horrible memories kept flooding back beneath the polite attempts at conversation.

No, I am not going to do Christmas again, I'll hide indoors until it is all over.

**

The winter has been so dead this year. The sparrows have been sitting in the bush by their feeding station all puffed up and ragged looking. Usually in Mother's garden there is something blooming bravely through the mild Cornish winter, but not this year. The bullocks have gone from the hill and the plum trees have looked like dead twigs. Her potted camellias, nurtured for years with copious amounts of fertilizer and covered with old net curtains to protect them from the frost, have died one by one until there are none left.

But now the garden is waking up. The flower buds are showing on the Daffodils, Snowdrops line the bank of the stream, there is a mass of purple Hellebore by the old steps and there are catkins on the Hazel. The bullocks are back. The thrush is grooming itself and splashing about in the bird bath. I think perhaps it is time to scatter Mother's ashes.

**

Most of the tribe were here yesterday for the scattering of ashes and it turned out to be quite a jolly affair with plenty of hugs and chatterings. Our little kitchen table was laden with contributions of the sticky, sweet and definitely unhealthy type of celebratory food and despite gathering every chair from every room to join the outdoor furniture on the patio, there was standing room only for some. It was comforting to watch the three generations of us occupying Mother's garden in the sunshine, weaving past the fruit trees, toddling down the stone path, kneeling on the bridge to watch the stream gurgling beneath and laughing and reminiscing on the patio.

I have been puzzling for ages about exactly how to do the ashes, particularly as I had been told by the funeral director to be careful not to throw the ashes into the air as they would be very light and blow about in the slightest movement of air. I'm glad I didn't have to organise a sky burial or a funeral pyre, this one should be simple. In the morning I decided to put the ashes in a tube, so that they could be released near to the water's surface by someone kneeling on the bridge, and I found a cardboard tube from some of Mother's old Christmas wrapping paper and covered it with a decorative paper. It was Roz and I that had the task of transferring the large bag of ashes into the tube. It was one of the most bizarre things I've ever done and I am afraid we couldn't help but laugh at the absurdity of what we were doing; it was so odd, comedic, opening the bag of tiny white flakes, like an ingredient for baking, and poring out Mother, but not Mother, into the tube. The long tube filled up and became heavy and a thin cloud of barely visible fine ash puffed into the air. I couldn't avoid breathing it in.

There was no cue, no call for action, but somehow everybody had gathered on the bridge and down each side of the stream. As Mother's ashes slid out of the tube and clouded the water there was a multitude of individual goodbyes, laden with love and gratitude but not with sadness.

I kept some of the ashes back because I decided after all to bury some in the garden. I wasn't afraid any more that she would keep an eye on me when I was doing the gardening; that was something that belonged to this world and I was sure that where ever she was she would feel quiet and peaceful. So when everybody had left I went alone to the bottom of the garden and dug a small hole at the base of a little tree that Mother's sisters had given her and poured some of the ashes in there. The robin came while I was doing it and he sat up in his usual tree and started his evening song, so sharp and powerful it cut through the air. Perhaps he had come to say farewell to Mother since she had cared for her garden birds, his ancestors, so well over many years.

Then I sat on the bench and dropped all that was left into the stream and watched as the white ashes sank into the current or spread over the surface of the water and tumbled around the bubbles and flurries as the motion of the stream took them away. This really is goodbye. She is leaving me and her garden and her little house and her tribe of descendants and is on her way to the sea.